D0666364

INTIMATE FATHERS

Intimate Fathers

The Nature and Context of
Aka Pygmy Paternal Infant Care

BARRY S. HEWLETT

Ann Arbor

THE UNIVERSITY OF MICHIGAN PRESS

First paperback edition 1992

Copyright © by the University of Michigan 1991

All rights reserved

Published in the United States of America by

The University of Michigan Press

Manufactured in the United States of America

1994   1993   1992   4   3   2

Library of Congress Cataloging-in-Publication Data

Hewlett, Barry S., 1950–
    Intimate fathers : the nature and context of Aka pygmy paternal
infant care / Barry S. Hewlett.
        p.   cm.
    Includes bibliographical references and index.
    ISBN 0-472-10184-6 (cloth : alk. paper) — ISBN 0-472-08203-5
(paper : alk. paper)
    1. Aka (African people)—Families.   2. Father and child—Central
African Republic.   3. Central African Republic—Social life and
customs.   I. Title.
DT546.345.A35H48   1991
306.85′089965096741—dc20   90-48843
                                                             CIP

British Library Cataloguing in Publication Data

Hewlett, Barry S.
    Intimate fathers : the nature and context of Aka Pygmy
    paternal infant care.
    1. Africa. Children. Interpersonal relationships with
    fathers
    I. Title
    306.8742096

    ISBN 0-472-10184-6
    ISBN 0-472-08203-5

DT
546.345
.A35
H48
1992

For my wife, Cheri, and children,
David, Forrest, Allison, and Erika

Acknowledgments

It is a pleasure to gratefully acknowledge the generous assistance of the numerous individuals who have contributed significantly to my work with the Aka over the past fifteen years. My greatest debt is to the Aka; they made fieldwork fun and productive. They graciously opened up their daily life to the often strange work of the anthropologist—impersonal behavioral observations and lengthy interviews about their family life. I am especially grateful to the following Aka who provided extraordinary time and thought to my work: Luma, Boseke, Etobe, Mosala, Ikpada, Mbalika, Miya, Milalou, and Galo. A number of local farmers also assisted tremendously. Justin Mongosso has been a long-term friend and field assistant and has helped me in innumerable ways to ensure my physical and emotional well-being. Sebastian Zikobo and Edward Mboula also assisted my work in Bokoka. Local officials have been especially warm and receptive to my work, especially A. Mongosso, the Mayor of the Rural Community of Moboma, and Francois Bianzo, the Canton of Ndélé.

I would like to acknowledge and sincerely thank the government of the Central African Republic, especially Jean-Claude Kazagui, le Haut Commissaire de la Recherche Scientifique et Technologique, for providing the authorization to conduct the research. Mr. Kazagui is an exceptional government official—he took the time to have lengthy discussions about my work and provided efficient and rapid authorization to help encourage the research. I would also like to thank the members of the U.S. Embassy in Bangui, especially Katherine Montgomery and Fred LaSor, for going out of their way to provide hospitality and services.

For reading most of the manuscript at one stage or another and giving me their help and encouragement, I am most grateful to Napoleon Chagnon, Luca Cavalli-Sforza, Serge Bahuchet, P. Herbert Leiderman, Michael Jochim, Colin Turnbull, James Woodburn, Robert Bailey, Nadine Peacock, David Brokensha, Donald Symons, Michael Lamb, William Jankowiak, Suzanne Long, Robert Moise, Marion McCreedy, Art Lehmann, Carol Mukhopadhyay, Jean Hudson, Michelle Kisliuk, Elizabeth Watts, and Barbara Smuts.

The research was supported by the Wenner-Gren Foundation, the University of California Humanities Fund, and the Swan Fund. I am grateful to all those who made these awards possible. I would also like to acknowledge the permission by Erlbaum to reprint parts of an earlier article on Aka fathers (Hewlett 1987).

I am especially grateful and indebted to my parents, Harold and June Hewlett, who, despite all of their doubts, made a tremendous commitment to my work in Africa. Finally, this work would not have been possible without the patience, concern, careful reading, and assistance of my wife Cheri.

Contents

CHAPTER 1

Introduction

Despite a steady increase in the quantity and quality of studies of infants in non-Western populations (Munroe and Munroe 1971; Konner 1977; Chisholm 1983; Super and Harkness 1982), there are few detailed ethnographic studies of the father-infant relationship in these populations. Theoretical orientations, field methodologies and the nature of father-infant interaction have resulted in an emphasis on mother's role and a lack of data and understanding of father's role. Mother-oriented theories of infant and child development have guided cross-cultural research. The theories of child development of Ainsworth (1967), Bowlby (1969), Freud (1938), and Harlow (1961), which have generated much of the cross-cultural research, all view the mother-infant relationship as the prototype for subsequent attachments and relationships. According to Freud and Bowlby, for instance, one had to have a trusting, unconditional relationship with his or her mother in order to become a mentally healthy adult. These influential theorists generally believed that the father's role was not a factor in the child's development until the Oedipal stage (three to five years old). The field methods to study infancy cross-culturally reflected this theoretical emphasis on mother. Behavioral observations were either infant or mother-focused and conducted only during daylight hours; father-focused and evening observations were not made. The mother or infant-focused daylight observations thus neglected the father's care of other children and the father's activities with his own infant in the early evening hours before bed or during the night. Also, standardized questionnaires and psychological tests were generally administered only to mothers. One consistent result from the cross-cultural studies was that fathers provide substantially less direct care to infants than mothers. In fact, all cross-cultural studies to date indicate that a number of other female caretakers (older female siblings, aunts, grandmothers) provide more direct care to infants than do fathers. Since fathers are not as conspicuous as mothers and other females during daylight hours, researchers tend to emphasize a "deficit" model of fathers (Cole and Bruner 1974). The researchers do not know much about the father's role and therefore simply claim that it is minimal. These factors have contributed to the complete absence of systematic studies in non-Western societies of the father's role in infant and child development.

Given the paucity of systematic research in non-Western societies on father-infant interaction and on the father's role in the stages of child development, it is ironic that this variable (i.e., the degree of father vs. mother involvement with children) should be so consistently invoked as an explanatory factor in the literature. It is hypothesized to be related, for example, to universal sexual asymmetry (Rosaldo and Lamphere 1974); variations in sexual dimorphism (Wilson 1975); the origins of the human family (Lancaster and Lancaster 1987); male and female reproductive strategies (Draper and Harpending 1982); contemporary patterns of gender-activity differentiation (Brown 1970; Burton, Brudner, and White 1977); the association of males with culture and females with nature (Ortner 1974); smooth functioning of the family (Zelditch 1955); and proper moral development (Hoffman 1981).

Active father involvement with offspring is also implicated in gender-differentiated personality, cognitive and other social-behavioral traits in U.S. studies. The father's role in child-rearing, for example, is linked to high achievement in females (Block, van der Lippe and Block 1973) and higher performance on cognitive tasks, particularly spatial tasks (Radin 1981), and the presence of an analytical cognitive style in both girls and boys (Witkin and Berry

1975). Father absence, in contrast, is associated with aggressive and violent behavior among adolescent males, particularly in the United States (Anderson 1968; Bacon, Child, and Barry 1963; Siegman 1966; Whiting 1965). This is generally attributed to male sexual identity problems arising from the lack of a suitable masculine role model during the formative stages. Father absence has also been suggested to produce authoritarian, dominant, egotistic behavior in boys in other cultural settings, with the warning that one must control for the effects of family task assignments (Ember 1973). Finally, the father's degree and style of child-rearing involvement is thought to be related to self-esteem (Sears 1970) and social confidence (Fish and Biller 1973).

Other purportedly universal gender-differentiated personality traits are attributed to female predominance and male absence in child-rearing. Chodorow (1973), for example, focuses on a young boy's relative lack of exposure to his father. This produces, she argues, a perception of manhood that necessitates the rejection of women and of things symbolizing femininity, such as infant care. Women, in contrast, acquire their sexual identity more easily and directly, by observing their mothers. As a result, women are less individuated than men, have more flexible ego boundaries, and are more dependent and relational. Rosaldo (1974), building on Chodorow, postulates additional orientations in women that arise from the female reproductive role: particularistic versus universalistic orientation; vertical rather than horizontal interpersonal ties; and an experientially generated affinity toward ascribed rather than achieved status.

Anthropologists and psychologists have theorized extensively on how the father's role influences behavior without the benefit of systematic studies of the father's role in non-Western populations. This study was stimulated, in part, by the general lack of data on the father's role in non-Western settings and the resulting "deficit" model of the father's role, but also by the results of psychologists' studies of fathers in the United States. Extensive psychological research on the American father-infant relationship has consistently demonstrated that fathers are more likely than mothers to engage in vigorous play with the infant (Arco 1983; Belsky 1980; Clarke-Stewart 1978; Crawley and Sherrod 1984; Field 1978; Lamb 1976, 1977a, 1985; Parke and O'Leary 1976; Yogman 1982; but see Pederson, Anderson, and Cain 1980, for an exception). An American father's vigorous play with the infant is evident three days after birth and continues throughout infancy. The American data have been so consistent that some researchers have indicated a biological origin (Clarke-Stewart 1980). The function of the father's physically stimulating play with the infant is suggested to be the critical means by which father-infant attachment is established and the initial means by which the infant learns social competence (Lamb 1981). Mother-infant attachment develops as a consequence of the frequency and intensity of the relationship, while the infant's attachment to the father occurs as a result of the highly stimulating interaction. Since mothers and fathers represent different styles of interaction, infants are likely to develop differential expectations of them, which in turn increases the infants' awareness of different social styles. Later in childhood, it is suggested, it is primarily the father who introduces the child into the public sphere. These functional differences in parenting style are suggested as support of the expressive/instrumental role theory first introduced by Durkheim (1933) and elaborated by Parsons and Bales (1955). According to this theory, the male role is primarily "instrumental": oriented to the external world and responsible for helping the child establish ties with individuals outside the family (i.e., social competence). In contrast, the female role is "expressive": responsible for the emotional and affective climate of the home, the nurturance of the young, and domestic tasks.

The few observational studies conducted in industrialized nations outside the United States have questioned the universality of the American data. Swedish fathers play slightly more with their infants than do Swedish mothers, yet the distinctive physical style of American fathers does not exist (Lamb et al. 1982). Swedish infants demonstrate significantly more attachment toward mothers than toward fathers (Lamb et al. 1983), whereas American infants exhibit no such preference (Lamb 1976, 1977b). This fits the theoretical model mentioned above—if Swedish fathers do not provide distinctive playfulness, they will not become as affectively salient as the primary caretaking mothers. German fathers observed with their newborns in the mothers' hospital rooms also do not exhibit this stimulating playfulness (Parke, Grossman, and Tinsley 1981). Although the American studies of fathers are remarkably consistent, the few European studies suggest that more extensive cross-cultural research is essential to understanding the father's role in infant development.

This study extends our understanding of the father's role by examining father-infant interaction among the Aka Pygmy hunter-gatherers of Central Africa. The Aka are exceptional in comparison to other societies in that fathers are actively involved with infants and are second only to mothers in the amount of direct care to their infants. My ethnographic work with the Aka began in 1973, but I did not start to systematically study fathers' roles until 1984. After living with the Aka on and off for ten years, I recognized that Aka fathers were exceptionally close to their infants, but this did not seem remarkable as they were exceptionally close to everyone in camp (see pl. 1). I never considered a study of fathers' roles until I read some of the Western psychological literature on fathers' roles while working as a health coordinator for a child development agency. My subjective observations of Aka fathers were inconsistent with the broad characterizations of fathers' roles described in the psychological literature. I had no idea that Aka fathers would turn out to be unique by cross-cultural standards.

My overall aim was to describe in quantitative and qualitative detail the nature of Aka father-infant interaction, and to relate this interaction to biological, ecological, demographic, social, and ideological constraints. I was interested in identifying factors that might explain the nature of and intracultural variability in the Aka father-infant relationship. Numerous types of data could have been collected on Aka fathers, however, I emphasized the father's level of involvement and style of interaction (as compared to the mother's and others'). Primary questions investigated within each of these areas are listed below:

1. Degree of paternal involvement
   a) How often do fathers actually interact with their infants?
   b) How often are fathers available to their infants?
   c) If fathers are not involved with infants, what other activities are they involved in?
   d) How do children characterize the nature of their involvement with their fathers?
2. Paternal versus maternal parenting style
   a) Are there distinctions between the mother's and the father's play behavior with their infants?
   b) Do mothers and fathers hold their infants for different purposes?
   c) What do mothers and fathers do while they hold the infant?
   d) Do infants show different types of attachment behavior to mothers and fathers?
   e) How do children view their mother's and father's parenting styles?

TERMINOLOGY

Before detailing the nature of the father's role among the Aka, it would be useful to define some basic terms.

The terms *involvement* and *investment* are often used interchangeably, but in this study father *involvement* is emphasized and is considered only one type of father's *investment*. Father involvement is any active or passive care of the infant. Holding, feeding, grooming, cleaning, and playing are types of active involvement while touching and being within one meter or within view of the infant are considered passive types of involvement. These passive forms of involvement are sometimes called proximity maintenance behaviors. The father is available to the infant and can provide help if the infant is hurt, can keep the infant out of danger (e.g., keep from crawling into the fire or touching hot items), and can provide a model for the infant to learn particular tasks. Investment refers to a much broader range of the father's activities and is considered any kind of action or behavior that will increase the fitness of offspring. Generally, two types of investment are recognized—direct and indirect (Kleiman and Malcolm 1981). Direct investment refers to male activities and behaviors that have an immediate physical influence on infants' survival. Direct investment could include direct caregiving, providing food, actively transmitting subsistence skills and other cultural knowledge, keeping close to watch, protect and train the infant, and giving land or other goods at the time of the child's marriage or time of the father's death (i.e., inheritance). Indirect forms of investment are father's activities that benefit the child but that the father would do regardless of the child's presence. Types of indirect investment would include defending and maintaining access to important food resources, providing mother with economic or emotional support, and providing the child with an extensive kin network (i.e., the size of the father's kin group influences the child's survival).

The term *involvement* is used primarily by psychologists because they are interested in the emotional, cognitive, and social outcomes of father presence or absence. For instance, psychologists are interested in how father involvement influences male and female sexual identity, personality, moral and cognitive development. Evolutionary biologists, on the other hand, use the term *investment* to determine how fathers or males (they are interested in cross-species applications of their theories), contribute to the physical survival of their offspring. Unlike the psychologists, they are interested in all types of male investment, not only the direct care of the child. While this study emphasizes father involvement, it is important to recognize that fathers can and do contribute to their children in many different ways. Paternal investment in humans will be discussed at length in chapter 8.

Social scientists often distinguish biological and social fatherhood. Social fatherhood implies that fathers' relationships with their children are learned and socially rather than biologically determined. Social and cultural anthropologists who have worked with Australian aborigines and polyandrous societies have been especially influential in establishing the importance of social fatherhood. Australian aborigine groups do not emphasize the sexual act as the cause of pregnancy; spirit children in the natural environment enter the woman and are the primary cause of pregnancy, not the man's semen. In polyandrous societies two or more men, usually brothers, have a wife in common and all of the husbands are called father by the children. The importance of biological fatherhood in these societies is minimized in their cultural ideologies. Also, anthropologists have pointed out that in many, if not most, societies around the world, the biological father as well as the father's brother and possibly other males are called "father" in the kinship terminology. I agree that humans are exceptional in their abilities to learn and move in and out of social roles, that is, expected behavior patterns, obligations, and privileges, but this does not mean that biology does not influence those roles. Social and legal institutions in many societies suggest an interest in biological paternity. This book does not distinguish between biological and social fatherhood because it is so difficult to separate the two. Both biological and cultural factors are considered in an attempt to understand Aka father-infant relations. I am reasonably certain that the Aka males in this study are the biological fathers of the infants in the study. Genetic studies indicate that over 90 percent of the time there is agreement between Aka biological and social paternity (Cavalli-Sforza 1986). It is important to remember that humans do have a few exceptional, although probably not exclusive, characteristics—social fatherhood is one of them. Social fatherhood has contributed to the pronounced cross-cultural diversity in the father's role.

Finally, there are a number of anthropological terms that are used to describe different subsistence patterns. The Aka subsist primarily on wild foods and are called hunter-gatherers, foragers (i.e., mobile rather than sedentary hunter-gatherers) or a band level society. The

Ngandu are the neighbors of the Aka and subsist primarily on a variety of domestic plants and animals and are called farmers, villagers, or a tribal level society.

THE ORGANIZATION OF THE BOOK

This book is a traditional anthropological approach to understanding human behavior. The preceding paragraphs have introduced the problem—potential Western bias in research on father's role. The next chapter provides a holistic description of a non-Western culture, the Aka, that will be used to test the validity of the Western psychological notions about father's role. Chapters 3 through 6 detail the methods and results of the specific field study of father's role among the Aka. Once the nature and context of father's role among the Aka has been established, Aka fathers are then compared to fathers in cultures around the world in chapter 7. Anthropologists have a strong conviction that before making a statement about human behavior, in this case father's role, one must examine that behavior in comparative perspective. Anthropologists also have a long-standing interest in understanding human behavior through time—not just the last few hundred years, but back millions of years, to the time of the earliest humans. Chapter 8, therefore, examines father's role over the course of human evolution. Finally, anthropologists tend to think that their studies of remote, so-called exotic populations can be useful for developing public policy in the West. Chapter 9 considers the implications of the Aka study of father's role for fathers in the United States.

Before examining one specific segment of Aka society in detail—the father-infant relationship—it is essential to have some sense of the environmental and social setting of Aka life. The father-infant relationship cannot be understood in isolation; environmental, cultural, and historical forces have all influenced the nature and context of the relationship. The next chapter is a brief sketch of the Aka natural and social environment, culture history, and basic aspects of Aka economic and social life.

CHAPTER 2

Aka Pygmies of the Western Congo Basin

The Aka Pygmies are foragers of the tropical forest regions of the southwestern Central African Republic (CAR) and northern People's Republic of the Congo (PRC) (see fig. 1). The Aka in this study are associated with the Bokoka section of Bangandu village (CAR). There are approximately 300 foraging Aka associated with Bokoka, and 769 farmers, primarily Ngandu peoples, in Bokoka.

NATURAL ENVIRONMENT

The most distinctive characteristic of the tropical rain forest is its great species richness; no other major ecological community has as many varieties of plants and animals (e.g., it has over 3,000 plant species) (Lewin 1986). Yet, the rain forest is a relatively poor place for foraging humans to live because animals are sparsely scattered and a low percentage of plants are edible (Dunn 1968; Richards 1973).

Ecology of the tropical rain forest is characterized by many species of plants and animals per unit area, but by few individuals per species in the same unit area. Ecologists sometimes describe the tropical forest as "marginal" by comparison to temperate environments, but the Aka certainly do not perceive their environment this way. It is seen as a plentiful environment, rich in game and edible plants. Nutritional studies coincide with Aka perceptions; Aka are

11

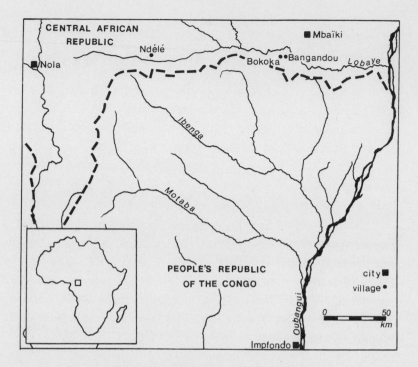

Fig. 1. General area occupied by Aka Pygmies and
location of study populations

better off than most other peoples of sub-Saharan Africa (Pennetti, Sgaramella-Zonta, and Astolfi 1986; Cordes and Hewlett 1990). But it is most likely the great accumulation of hunting and gathering knowledge and skill of the Aka that enables them to have a relatively abundant life in the forest.

Unlike Turnbull's (1965b) homogeneous portrayal of the Ituri forest, the western Congo Basin forest of the CAR and PRC is quite heterogeneous. There are at least eleven distinct ecological zones within the tropical forest occupied by the Aka (Bahuchet and Guillaume 1982). There are several types of solid ground (terra firma), semideciduous forests that are categorized according to subsoil type (e.g., secondary sandstone, tertiary sandstone or alluvia, quartzite sandstone, etc.), as well as a solid ground evergreen forest where *Gilbertiodendron* species are dominant. Most of the tropical forest is covered by the solid ground semideciduous forests, and within them one finds the primary species of hunted game: several species of duikers and red hogs occupy the ground level (along with the less frequently hunted gorilla and chimpanzee), while several species of monkeys (mangabeys, guenons, colobi), squirrels, and birds occupy the canopy. In the solid ground evergreen forest, one type of duiker (*Cephalophus leucogaster*) and the bongo antelope (*Boocercus euryceros*) are commonly hunted.

In the flat and riverine valleys that traverse the western Congo Basin there are swamp or marsh forests. The forest vegetation in the swamp varies according to the wetness and flooding of the land: In areas that are continuously flooded one encounters a low dense evergreen forest; on soils that are permanently damp, but only occasionally covered by water, a high canopied forest exists; and, in areas where flooding occurs periodically but where drainage is good so soils can eventually dry out, one finds a mixed forest. Wildlife of the swamp forests is also markedly different than that found in the solid ground forest. For instance, the largest mammals hunted by the Aka, the elephant and situtunga (*Tragelphus spekei*), are generally found in the swamp forest (Bahuchet and Guillaume 1982; Hewlett 1977).

Also, within the forest are pockets of naturally occurring open savannah as well as stretches of secondary forest (areas that have been abandoned by slash and burn farmers and that are characterized by a large number of vines and heliophilous trees, such as the Musanga umbrella tree). The fauna in these environments are distinct from those found in the swamp or solid ground forest. In the secondary forest Aka hunt for civet, numerous rats, and a few species of duiker (Bahuchet and Guillaume 1982; Hewlett 1977).

The climate of the Congo Basin is generally warm and humid. There are two seasons: a long rainy season and a dry season with much milder rains. On average, it rains 117 days per year for a total of 1,766 mm of rainfall (range is 1,407–2,381 mm) (Bahuchet

1985). August, September, and October are the wettest months, each averaging 230 mm of rainfall. The commencement of the seasons varies from year to year, but the rainy season generally begins in the first half of March and the dry season generally begins in November.

While there is marked variation in the seasons, there is little variation in the temperature throughout the year. The mean temperature during the year is 24.5 degrees C, but the difference between the high temperature of the warmest month (March) and the high temperature of the coldest month (July) is only 2 degrees C. The difference between the monthly average high temperature and monthly average low temperature also varies slightly during the year; the greatest difference in high and low temperature is 11.8 degrees C (February). The relative humidity is also comparatively constant, averaging 92.4 percent at 7:00 A.M. and 69.6 percent at midday (Deuss 1968; Bahuchet 1985).

CULTURAL HISTORY

There is considerable debate over the prehistory of African Pygmies. Ethnohistoric (Schebesta 1933; Turnbull 1983), linguistic (Bahuchet 1985, 1987), and genetic (Cavalli-Sforza 1986) data suggest a long history of independent occupation of the forest by Pygmies until the Bantu expansion about 2,000 years ago (David 1980; Phillipson 1980). Recent ecological studies (Hart and Hart 1986; Bailey et al. 1989) question this interpretation and instead hypothesize that the Pygmies (or any other forest foraging population) could not have subsisted in the interior regions of the forest without entering into a symbiotic relationship with farmers to obtain carbohydrates. These researchers suggest the forest does not yield enough carbohydrates (specifically, wild yams) for people to live there independently. They hypothesize that Pygmies originally lived on the margins of the forest exploiting both forest and savannah habitats and did not move into the forest until forest farmers moved in with them. Archaeological evidence for their hypothesis does not exist as archaeological data are extremely limited in the African tropical forest. In the CAR numerous surface collections along forest rivers have produced artifacts of great antiquity (e.g., Acheulean hand axes) (Bayle des Hermes 1973), but no stratified archaeological sites have been excavated in the forest interior (van Noten 1982).

The ethnohistoric accounts of Pygmies go back thousands of years. Pharaoh Phiops II of the 6th Dynasty (about 2300 B.C.) mentions a Pygmy dancer brought back from an expedition to the forest, while Homer, Herodotus, and Aristotle are but a few others to mention Pygmies or small African people, often called Aka (see Tyson in Windle 1894 for early citations of Pygmies). Although these early reports are very vague concerning the location of the Pygmies, they are cited (Schebesta 1933; Turnbull 1983) as evidence to support the contention that Pygmies lived in the forest before the Bantu expansion.

Little is mentioned of Pygmies between the fourth century and 1850. Most references during this period refer only to their mythological existence. George Schweinfurth in 1870 was the first European to rediscover the Pygmies, and shortly thereafter Miani (Giglioli 1880) and Stanley (1891) confirmed the existence of forest Pygmies, Miani being influential in getting two Pygmies back to Italy.

The colonial period was a time of dramatic change for the Aka. The European and American demand for slaves, ivory, wild rubber, and duiker skins affected their forest life. To flee Dutch slave traders in the 1700s the Ngandu farmers, the horticulturalists with whom the Aka of Bokoka live in association today, moved northward from the Imfondo area of the PRC and settled on the southern banks of the Lobaye. This movement of peoples must have increased the population density of the region and the number of farmers desiring the meat and services of the Aka. Resulting changes in Aka social organization are difficult if not impossible to reconstruct for this early period. At the end of the nineteenth century ivory became the major export from the region, and the Aka were the principal producers. Villagers were responsible for providing the ivory to colo-

15

nial traders but it was usually the Aka, armed with spears and sometimes guns, who killed the elephants to acquire the ivory. This development increased the frequency and type of exchange between farmers and Aka, depleted the elephant population, and promoted the *tuma* (great elephant hunter) to greater social status. After 1908, the number of guns increased and the number of elephants decreased, and the European concessions in the region became interested in rubber. During a period of wild rubber exploitation (1910 to 1940), European agents employed "forced labor" regulations to get male farmers to go into the forest and drain trees of rubber. While the Aka were never employed to collect rubber, the farmers' demands on them for meat increased because male farmers could not do any of their own hunting. I have collected a number of accounts from this period in which villagers fled the forced labor situation to live in remote areas of the forest with Aka. The farmer's family would make a garden in a remote forest area where Aka hunted and gathered. By 1925 a market for duiker skins developed in France to make coats and chamois leather. The market peaked in the 1950s when 27,000 duiker skins per year were being exported from some forest areas (Dongier 1953). This encouraged Aka to use nets more often than the traditional spear hunting. Today, Aka and farmers in the CAR say that net hunting was traditionally a villager hunting technique, and that spear hunting was the primary hunting technique of the Aka. But a greater demand for meat by villagers during the forced labor period and the European market for duiker skins prompted the Aka to adopt net hunting. The decision to net hunt affected Aka social organization: The social status of *tuma* decreased while that of the *nganga* (traditional healer who also directs hunting rituals and practices divination on the net hunt) increased, and the sharing of meat became less egalitarian (duiker meat is not divided among all members of the camp as is elephant or red hog meat). In the 1930s the French attempted a "taming policy" to integrate the Aka into the colonial system by encouraging them to move onto the roads and begin farming, but few Aka complied, and the policy's influence seems limited to a few areas in the PRC (Bahuchet and Guillaume 1982; Bahuchet 1985).

Today the Aka continue to be affected by the world economy. In Bokoka, for instance, the Aka move into the village for part of the dry season, at the expense of missing the best net hunting of the year, to help the farmers with their coffee plantations. The coffee, destined for the European market, is the primary means by which villagers acquire money. Some Aka help villagers hunt elephant for ivory, while other Aka work for lumber companies in the region.

The history of the area has also contributed to linguistic diversity. There are approximately fifteen ethnic groups who speak fifteen languages and live in association with the approximately 30,000 Aka in the CAR and the PRC. The Aka language is a distinct Bantu language and is classified in the C-10 Bantu language group, belonging to the Benue-Congo group of the Niger Congo, a subdivision of the Congo-Kordofanian phylum (Greenberg 1963). Unlike the Mbuti Pygmies in the Ituri who speak the same language as their village neighbors (Turnbull 1965b), the Aka speak their own language (*diaka*), as well as the language of their neighbors.

DEMOGRAPHY

To demonstrate both variation and continuity of demographic features within Aka society two locations will be compared: Bokoka, where the father-infant study was conducted, and Ndélé, about 125 km west of Bokoka. The demographic data are based upon a population of 283 Aka from Bokoka and 274 Aka from Ndélé. One regional variation that should be kept in mind when interpreting the demographic data is the difference in population density: the population density in Bokoka is about twice the population density of Ndélé (0.33 persons/km^2 in Bokoka and 0.17 persons/km^2 in Ndélé) (Cavalli-Sforza 1986). Besides demonstrating the demographic variability within Aka culture, comparisons with !Kung San and Yanomamö demographic data are also made.

17

Table 1 describes the sex-age structure of the Aka from Bokoka and Ndélé and compares the Aka structure with that of the !Kung San and Yanomamö. Aka data from the two locations are remarkably similar, and the Aka population structure is much closer to that of the Yanomamö than that of the !Kung San.

Fertility is high and infertility infrequent. The total fertility rate (TFR) or mean number of live births for postmenopausal women is approximately 5.5. Neuwelt-Truntzer (1981) estimated 5.1 live births for Aka women from Zomia; Cavalli-Sforza (1986) found an average of 5.0 live births for women from various areas in the Central African Republic, while Aka women associated with Bokoka averaged 6.2 live births and Aka women in Ndélé averaged 5.6 live births. The completed fertility of Aka females lies between the 4.7 live births found with !Kung San females (Howell 1979) and the 7.9 live births found with Yanomamö women (Early and Peters 1990).

Female infertility is rare among the Aka; only one woman was reported infertile. All women get married, generally by sixteen to seventeen years of age. Men first marry two to four years later than women.

Male reproductive histories were also recorded. As expected, Bokoka and Ndélé men over forty-five years of age averaged almost the same number of live births as postmenopausal Aka women from the area. But unlike the Aka women, the men had greater reproductive variability (e.g., Bokoka male variance = 8.64 while female variance = 5.20). Some Aka men had no children while others had fourteen, whereas all Aka women had at least two children, but none had more than eleven. This pattern of greater male variability is consistent with that found among the !Kung San (Howell 1979) and Yanomamö (Chagnon 1979).

The birth interval of Aka women from Bokoka averaged 3.5 years while women from Ndele averaged 3.7 years. This is somewhat lower than the 4.2 years calculated by Neuwelt-Truntzer (1981) for the Aka from Zomia and the 4-year interval found among the !Kung San (Howell 1979) but is substantially higher than the 2.9-year interval estimated for the Yanomamö (Melancon 1981).

18

Infant mortality is also high. Retrospective life histories of women indicate an infant (up to twelve months) mortality rate of 20 percent, which is slightly below the 22 percent infant mortality rate estimated by Neuwelt-Truntzer (1981) for the Aka of Zomia. Aka infant mortality is essentially indistinguishable from the infant mortality rates of the !Kung (20.2 percent [Howell 1979]) and the Yanomamö (21.8 percent [Early and Peters 1990]).

A causes of death study (Hewlett, van de Koppel, and van de Koppel 1986) identified the major cause of Aka death at all ages—infectious and parasitic diseases. Accidental and violent deaths were relatively infrequent especially in comparison with the Yanomamö and !Kung San. The causes of death study also indicated that males at every age were at greater risk of death than were females. Young adult males (eighteen to twenty-five years) were at especially high risk relative to female risk of death at the same age. This pattern is consistent with that found among the Yanomamö (Melancon 1981) and !Kung San (Howell 1979).

Table 2 examines the polygyny and divorce rates for Ndélé and Bokoka Aka. Again, they are very similar, about 17 percent of Aka men have more than one wife, and about one of four marriages

TABLE 1. Sex and Age Distribution, in Percentage

	Ndélé Aka	Bokoka Aka	!Kung[a]	Yanomamö[b]
Age in Years				
0–14	42.0	44.5	28.9	45.4
15–29	22.6	23.7	24.6	30.1
30–44	20.0	17.3	24.9	16.3
45–59	9.8	8.5	13.4	7.2
> 60	5.5	6.0	8.2	1.0
Sex ratio (m/f)				
Less than 15				
years old	1.2	1.2	0.8	1.3
Greater than				
15 years old	0.9	0.7	0.9	1.0

[a]Howell 1979
[b]Chagnon 1968

19

TABLE 2. Aka Polygyny and Divorce Rates

	Percentage of Males Having			Divorce Rate		
	1 wife	2 wives	3 wives	No. of Marriages[a]	No. of Divorces	Rate (in %)
Ndélé Aka	82.6	13.8	3.6	206	53	25.7
Bokoka Aka	82.1	16.1	1.8	195	56	28.7

[a]number of male and female marriages

ends in divorce. Most of the divorces come at an early age before children are born. Most of the early divorces are initiated by women, whereas most divorces after age thirty-five (when women have completed fertility) are initiated by men.

Overall, the age-sex structure, fertility, and mortality patterns are consistent with those in other hunter-gatherer and horticultural populations. Both fertility and mortality are high and the population is relatively young. The causes of death study indicates the Aka are more peaceful than many other hunter-gatherers and horticulturalists (Hewlett 1990).

SOCIAL UNITS

There are at least five significant social units: the family, the camp, the clan, the band, and the regional community. The family (husband, wife and children) is the most significant as this is the unit of production and reproduction: The family works as an economic unit on the net hunt, and in a variety of other subsistence activities (e.g., collecting caterpillars and mushrooms), and the conjugal family is where most cultural skills are transmitted and acquired (Hewlett and Cavalli-Sforza 1986). The camp (*lango*) consists of one to fifteen nuclear families but averages around twenty to thirty-five individuals. Table 3 compares the average size of forest and village camps in Ndélé and Bokoka. The data indicate there is no appreciable difference in the size of camps in the village and forest. There is no clear pattern of Aka concentration and dispersal as is found among many other foraging populations (Lee and DeVore 1968). There is a tendency for Bokoka forest camps to get larger during the dry season, as this is the best time for cooperative net hunting. Bahuchet (1985) points out that before 1900 Aka camps were concentrated during the dry season for net hunting and dispersed the rest of the year. While this tendency was found in Bokoka, it is quite variable from year to year. In Bokoka in 1980, for instance, there was a large measles epidemic, and most village camps during the dry season were large, but in 1984 village camps were small. In Ndélé, during the 1973 wet season, the Aka made large camps (greater than forty individuals) in the village, but in 1976 and 1980 the village camps were small (about twenty-five individuals). One pattern is clear: When Aka take up farming deep in the forest, the size of the camp grows appreciably. One Aka camp near Ndélé that had taken up farming numbered ninety-five, while another camp near Bokoka numbered sixty-seven.

The camp generally consists of three to four adult males from the same patriclan (usually brothers or first cousins), their wives and children, an elderly mother of some of the adult males, an older divorced sister of the patriclan and her children, a daughter of one of the adult males and her spouse who is performing bride service, and one or two visiting families. In Ndélé, 56 percent of the adult males in the camp belonged to the same patriclan, 19 percent of the males were in camp to do bride service, and 25 percent of the adult males were visiting. In Bokoka, the figures were 47 percent, 19 percent, and 33 percent, respectively.

TABLE 3. Camp Size in the Forest and Village

	No. of Camps	Mean	SD
Forest			
Ndélé	6	22.3	3.6
Bokoka	6	34.0	5.4
Village			
Ndélé	7	22.5	8.4
Bokoka	9	23.3	11.3

While the core of the camp usually consists of adult males belonging to the same patriclan (*dikanda*)—that is, individuals tracing their ancestry patrilineally to a mythical plant or animal, clan identity is weak. Few Aka know the mythology associated with their clan and Aka rarely invoke clan obligations if family members do not help out in subsistence activities. Aka adults can seldom remember patrilineal links back more than two generations and matrilineal relatives are visited frequently. An Aka male's clan name is the same as his Ngandu trading partner. Aka members of the Bodikala clan, for instance, usually trade with Ngandu farmers of the Bodikala clan. Consequently, Aka and Ngandu children grow up with their future trading partners. Table 4 lists the mean clan size from Ndélé and Bokoka. Tables 3 and 4 indicate that the mean clan size is not significantly different from the mean camp size.

The band is a more elusive entity as the Aka do not have a native term for it. Essentially it is a group of 50–150 individuals who hunt and gather in the same vicinity. Its core usually consists of two to four clans. There is general stability in the band over time. I have been returning to some areas for over fifteen years now and can generally take a trail to a particular territory and find many of the same individuals hunting and gathering together. Changes do of course occur. One camp or clan, for instance, may move to a new area because hunting is not good or the *konza* (village patron) is not treating them well or is running out of manioc. In Bokoka there were three bands, consisting of 65, 150, and 52 individuals, respectively, while in Ndélé the three bands consisted of 95, 125, and 50 individuals. Each band usually has one trail from the village to the forest camps.

The final social unit is the regional community or what in other

TABLE 4. Mean Clan Size in Ndélé and Bokoka

	No. of Clans	Mean	SD
Ndélé	6	19.5	5.6
Bokoka	7	22.7	6.2

publications is called the "exploration range" (Hewlett, van de Koppel, and Cavalli-Sforza 1982). This is the limited geographical area an individual explores during his or her lifetime. The "exploration range" is where subsistence activities take place, a spouse is encountered, and other aspects of geographical as well as social knowledge are acquired and transmitted. Aka tend to travel in a 50 km radius area from their place of birth (Hewlett, van de Koppel, and Cavalli-Sforza 1986) and get to know about 700 Aka in this area. In Ndélé, Aka males have a greater exploration range than females, and the Ndélé Aka also have a greater exploration range than Bokoka Aka. Population density is an important factor in how far one travels. Population density in Bokoka is twice that of Ndélé so Bokoka Aka do not have to travel as far to meet the same number of people. Male exploration range is also related to the distance traveled to find a spouse and helps to explain why Ndélé males travel farther than Ndélé women. The exploration range for Aka seems to approximate the dialectical tribe described by Birdsell (1973), in that it tends to include an area where one meets and gets to know about 500–700 individuals. The Aka have no term for the community of individuals one gets to know during his or her lifetime.

SUBSISTENCE AND SETTLEMENT

The Aka know hundreds of forest plants and animals but subsist primarily on sixty-three plant species, twenty insect species, honey from eight species of bees, and twenty-eight species of game. The Aka collect roots from six species of plants, leaves from eleven species, nuts from seventeen species, and fruits from seventeen species. They collect twelve species of mushrooms, four types of termites, crickets, three types of grubs, and twelve species of caterpillars. The Aka hunt seven species of large game with the spear (primarily hog and elephant), six species of duiker with the net (primarily the blue duiker), eight species of monkeys with the crossbow, and seven species of rat, mongoose, and porcupine with a

23

variety of small snare and net traps (see Bahuchet 1975, 1985, and Hewlett 1977 for details of plants and animals and associated hunting and collecting techniques).

The Aka clearly identify forest zones that are rich in particular plant or animal species. The best zone for caterpillar collecting, for instance, is about twelve km south of Bokoka. Specific zones of honey collection, roots, and *payo* nuts (*Irvingia* spp.) are identified within the hunting-gathering territory. Specific locations of the best duiker, pig, and elephant and bongo hunting are also well-known.

Over the course of a year the Aka spend about 56 percent of their time hunting, 27 percent of their time gathering, and 17 percent of their time in village work for the Ngandu (Bahuchet 1988). The relative importance of hunting and gathering activities fluctuates from season to season. It is estimated, for example, that the Aka spend up to 90 percent of their time net hunting in the drier season (January to May), while during part of the rainy season (August to September) 60 percent of their time is spent collecting food, especially caterpillars (Bahuchet 1988). Much of the vegetable food in the Aka diet is obtained by trading meat to farmers for manioc and other cultigens. Although the Aka net hunt in the forest the majority of the year and spend little or no time cultivating plant foods, they are transitional foragers in the sense that a large proportion of their diet comes from these domesticated village products. Seldom does a day go by without some of this food being eaten. While residing part of the year near the Ngandu village, Aka provide labor to their village *konza* (patron) for which they receive access to the farmer's fields. The Aka come to the village three or four months a year to assist in the clearing of the fields. A "typical" Aka meal in the dry season in a forest camp would consist of manioc, meat from a blue duiker cooked in a *payo* gravy, and shredded *koko* leaves (*Gnetum* spp.).

As with the Mbuti Pygmies of Zaire (Hart 1977; Turnbull 1965b), most camp members—male and female, young and old—participate in the net hunt (see pls. 2–4). From the time Aka leave the village and return to the forest (February-March) until caterpillar season (July-August), they often net hunt six days a week, four to nine hours per day. Net hunts decrease in frequency during the caterpillar season and the major rainy season (August-October); individual and small group foraging techniques (e.g., spears, crossbows, traps) are utilized more frequently during these seasons (see Bahuchet 1985 and Hewlett 1977 for descriptions of various hunting techniques). There are a few technical features about the net hunt that distinguish it from most other hunting techniques: There is no stalking of game; once the nets are set the object of the "beaters" is to make as much noise as possible in order to wake up the nocturnal duikers, the primary targets of the net hunt. It is also one of the few hunting techniques where ears are just as important as eyes and where women and children can contribute to the success of the hunt. There are at least six types of net hunt. Usually the nets are arranged in a semicircle and the men flush out the game and the women trap and kill it (this is the most common type of net hunt and called *banda*). In other instances the women are the beaters and the men the trappers (this type of net hunt is called *mbembo*).

Although both men and women collect leaves, fruits, nuts, mushrooms, and termites, women do the majority of the collecting. They may do this as a conjugal unit or individually. Men do the majority of the honey collecting, especially if it involves climbing a tree large in diameter. Both men and women net hunt, usually together, but sometimes individually, and men and women both use small traps to hunt, often together, but again, sometimes individually. Only men use the spear and crossbow to hunt.

Seasonal camp movements vary according to a variety of social and ecological factors. Most Aka associated with Bokoka move into the village from late November until mid-February, whereas Aka associated with Ndélé are in the village from August until October. Bokoka farmers are wealthier than the Ndélé farmers because the roads to Bokoka are better; they are also closer to urban areas (e.g., Bangui, the capital; and Mbaiki) and consequently have larger coffee plantations. The Aka in Bokoka move into the village during the early part of the dry season (December-January), when net hunting is best, to help villagers harvest their coffee. Aka are willing to do this because it is a time of plenty in the village; most of the yearly cash income for clothes, drink, and other commodities comes to the farmers during this period, and Aka reap some of those benefits. In Ndélé, on the other hand, coffee plantations are small and there is no caterpillar season (there is more swamp forest, which has fewer caterpillar trees), and consequently Aka move into the village during the height of the rainy season (August-October) rather than the dry season because net hunting is poorest at this time (the nets tear easily if wet).

There are some similarities in the seasonal movements of Ndélé and Bokoka Aka. Both Bokoka and Ndélé Aka are in the forest from March through June and July. Net hunting is good at this time and the trees start to flower, which means plenty of fruits, nuts (especially *payo*), and honey. Termites are also likely to swarm at this time. Aka are also less likely to obtain much from farmers at this time: May and June are the leanest times for villagers as they usually plant in April and hope to have their first crop by July.

SOCIAL ORGANIZATION

The Aka are patrilineal, having shallow patriclans (*dikanda*), and are generally virilocal except for a few years after marriage when the male provides bride service in the camp of his wife's family. Female lines are also recognized by the term *mobila*. This term refers to the lines of mother, mother's mother, father's mother, and father's mother's mother. Aka kinship terms are classificatory and basically generational; for instance, *tao* refers not only to the natural father but to the father's older brother and the husband of the mother's sister; and *ngue* (mother) refers to mother and mother's sister. All grandparents are called *koko*; all grandchildren are called *ndala*; all offspring are called *mona*; and all brothers and sisters are called *kadi*. *Mokio* refers to your spouse's mother's and father's family members, and *mokope* refers to all spouses of patriclan members.

26

Aka prefer to marry far away, and clan exogamy is practiced. Although Aka do not practice sister exchange as do the Efe Pygmies of Zaire, there is a tendency for males in one area to marry females from a particular location. In Ndélé, for instance, many of the men obtained wives from the Kaka region in the PRC. A man acquires a bride through service to his wife's family, often until the first infant of the married couple walks well. Men conducting bride service in the same camp usually become close friends for life. Bride service takes place regardless of the age of the woman, but as a woman gets older the length of bride service diminishes.

There are few Aka status positions. There is no chief in the sense of a person commanding ultimate authority, yet there is the *kombeti,* who is generally more influential in subsistence and camp movement discussions. He is often a liaison between Aka and Ngandu. The farmers show deference to the Aka *kombeti* (e.g., saying hello to him first, giving him more cigarettes) yet the Aka themselves do not show any such behavior toward him (intergenerational inequality is minimal). The *nganga* is the traditional healer and provides a wide range of services to the community—such as divination on hunts, curing of witchcraft, and herbal healing. The *tuma* is the great hunter who has often killed several elephants on his own. He leads spear hunts and important hunting and seasonal rituals and organizes the training of young boys in the men's secret society. The status positions are usually held by males.

The Aka are fiercely egalitarian and independent. No individual has the right to coerce or order another individual to perform an activity against his/her will. Even when parents give instructions to their children to collect water or firewood, there are no sanctions if they do not do so. Aka have a number of informal noninstitutional methods for maintaining their egalitarianism. First, they practice prestige avoidance; one does not draw attention to his or her activities. There are certainly exceptional hunters, dancers and drummers, but individuals do not brag to others about their abilities. Second, they practice the rough joking described by Lee (1986) among the !Kung San. For instance, if a man boasts about the

27

amount of honey he collected, others will joke about the size and shape of his genitals. And third, they practice demand sharing. This simply means that whatever one has will be given up if requested. This is one reason Aka have been slow to take up farming. An Aka who spends three to four months farming must give everything away at harvest time when all the relatives come to visit and request food.

Sharing, cooperation, and autonomy are but a few other of the Aka core values. The community cooperates daily in the net hunt, food hunted is shared with members of the camp, and decision-making is the reserved prerogative of the individual; if one is not content with living conditions, for instance, one moves to another camp. As a result, camp composition changes daily.

BELIEF SYSTEMS

Aka belief systems are best characterized by their regional and individual variation rather than by a standardized religious pattern. Unlike kinship terms, marriage rules, and social organization, where there is generally agreement between informants, there is consistent disagreement about the supernatural world. I would talk with a few informants about belief systems and begin to sketch out a general pattern, when the next informant would ridicule and clearly disagree with the earlier informants' statements. Although more research is needed in this area, a few general patterns eventually emerge.

The very individualistic nature of Aka beliefs is clearly demonstrated by some activities associated with adolescence. Aka circumcise boys at adolescence, and both boys and girls point their top four incisors (and possibly their bottom four) at this time (Walker and Hewlett 1989). The timing of these activities, however, is determined by the individual boy or girl. Whenever boys or girls feel like having their teeth pointed, a *tuma* is called in to point them. Adolescents decide if they want to have their teeth pointed with other male or female friends. The activities are very casual and individualized and contain a minimum amount of ritual. Aka male

28

and female initiations are considerably different from the male (*nkumbi*) and female (*elima*) adolescent initiations described by Turnbull (1965b) among the Mbuti Pygmies.

But similar to Turnbull's (1961) portrayal of the Mbuti, the Aka view the village (*mboka*) as a dangerous place, whereas the forest (*ndima*) is perceived as comforting and protecting. Aka express their fears about bad spirits and aggressive farmers in the village, and their demeanor in the village clearly communicates this fear. In the forest, Aka sing, dance, play, and are very active and conversant. In the village, their demeanor changes dramatically—they walk slowly, say little, seldom smile, and try to avoid eye contact with others. While camping in the plantations outside the village (*ngondu*), the Aka are more relaxed, but they still behave cautiously for a villager could overhear their conversations or enter the camp at any time.

Some Aka religious beliefs are similar to those of the Ngandu. Aka, like Ngandu, believe in ancestor spirits (*edio*). Aka generally recognize two types—personalized spirits (spirits that have names and belong to particular families) and nameless generalized spirits. An example of the first type of *edio* was provided by an Aka woman. She reported that the spirit of her dead husband knocked her new husband to the ground because the new husband married her too soon after her former husband's death. The degree and type of influence of *edio* in the daily life of Aka varies from one individual to the next. A few informants said all *edio* were bad, while others indicated they could help out on the hunt. Some Aka feel that they need to practice magic daily to protect themselves from *edio*, while others feel that *edio* have minimal influence in their life. Many Aka reported that *edio* could cause illnesses by sitting next to people and eating their food, so that they would eventually grow thin and die. Only an *nganga,* the traditional healer, had the ability to talk to *edio* to get them to leave.

Most Aka camps have an *nganga*. Ngangas can cure all forms of illness (e.g., malaria, worms, bad luck, attack by witchcraft), see into the future to help one make decisions about travel, marriage,

29

or friendships, and can see game animals deep in the forest while on the net hunt. There is tremendous intracultural variation in the abilities of the *ngangas*. Some are especially powerful and spend their time traveling from camp to camp to provide their services. The majority of *ngangas* are part-time practitioners and only have a few areas of specialization. *Ngangas* acquire their knowledge through training and initiation. During initiation, the insides of their eyelids are cut and medicine is placed in the cuts to help the *nganga*s see those things most others cannot. The number and importance of Aka *ngangas* are increasing as the number of Ngandu and other villager *ngangas* declines. Villager *ngangas* are increasingly difficult to find and can be very expensive so more villagers turn to Aka *ngangas*. Aka *ngangas* living near the village get a brisk business from villagers, who generally believe that Aka have supernatural abilities. Villagers are usually charged for their treatment (e.g., a chicken, a piece of cloth, salt, tobacco, etc.), while generally there is no charge for treating other Aka.

Also like Ngandu farmers, the Aka believe in witches (*limba*) and witchcraft (*gundu*). Aka from Ndélé attributed 15 percent of their parents' and children's deaths to witchcraft, while Bokoka Aka attributed only 7 percent of their deaths to witchcraft (Hewlett, van de Koppel, and van de Koppel 1986). The witches or sorcerers (the Aka make no distinction) practice secretly and are unknown to the general population, although *ngangas* are highly suspect. The witches send poison darts (*ndoki*) into the body of their victim, and the person eventually dies from the poison unless the *nganga* can extract the dart, usually by sucking it out.

Aka who believe in *bembe,* the creator of all living things, be lieve also that *bembe* retired soon after creation. The most consistently mentioned divinity or spirit is that of *dzengi,* a forest spirit. In the Bokoka region, *dzengi* is strongly associated with elephant hunting. One needs to dance and sing to *dzengi* to insure a successful elephant hunt. If an elephant is killed, a grand dance to *dzengi* is performed in which a large raffia mask symbolizing *dzengi* is utilized. The *dzengi* dance is organized and directed by the *tuma,* the great hunter.

All Aka adolescent boys are taken on an elephant hunt by a *tuma* to learn how to hunt elephant as well as to learn about the secret lore of *dzengi*. While women are kept peripheral to powers and secrets of *dzengi,* most women I spoke to about *dzengi* were not mystified or fearful of *dzengi* or the men's secrets, and in fact, sometimes laughed and said it was just a way the men tried to keep knowledge and power from them.

In Ndélé, *dzengi* was not specifically linked to the elephant hunt (although there would certainly be a dance to *dzengi* if an elephant was killed). In this region, one can dance to *dzengi* anytime the *tuma* agrees. As in Bokoka, the large raffia mask is used to symbolize *dzengi*. The *tuma* is bilingual and can communicate with the mask while it dances and translate *dzengi* messages to the others. The mask stops dancing when the singing and activity are poor or are not done with enough enthusiasm. The forest spirit likes singing, vigorous dancing, and play and will disappear if these behaviors are not exhibited. The *tuma* in Ndélé is also responsible for taking adolescent boys out on an elephant hunt to train them in the secret powers of *dzengi*.

Many Aka rituals are linked to hunting and gathering, and Aka engage in a number of individual and group hunting rituals to insure a successful hunt. To assist hunting efficiency the net can be ritually washed of bad spirits (*kose*) or a variety of medicines (*bouanga*) can be placed on them to increase good luck. The number and types of rituals increase as hunting success decreases (Moise 1987).

To this point, general features of Aka culture and environment have been described. They all have some effect on the nature of father-infant interaction. Precisely how these various aspects of Aka culture and environment are related to the father-infant relationship will be discussed in the following chapters. The next two topics of Aka culture—Aka infancy and husband-wife relations—are more central to father-infant relations. It is essential to have an understanding of Aka infancy and childhood and of gender relations to discuss the father-infant relationship.

AKA INFANCY AND CHILDHOOD

Infancy

There are various aspects of Aka infancy that contribute to and reflect the intimate nature of the father's role. The previous sections of this chapter provided some data on the physical and social setting of Aka infancy. In general, Aka infants live in small camps of twenty-five to thirty-five individuals. Half of the camp is under fifteen years of age and most adult women have a child under four years of age. Many of the other infants and children in camp are biologically related through the infant's father. The infant travels on the net hunt with the rest of the camp and sleeps in the same bed as its mother, father, and possibly older brothers and sisters. If a five-to-nine-year-old brother or sister has a grandparent (usually a grandmother) in camp, the child will sleep with the grandparent. After ten to eleven years of age girls often make their own house next to their parents, while boys will get together and make a lean-to in camp and all of them (two to four boys) will sleep together.

Aka infancy is indulgent: Infants are held almost constantly, they have skin-to-skin contact most of the day as Aka seldom wear shirts or blouses, and they are nursed on demand and attended to immediately if they fuss or cry. Aka parents interact with and stimulate their infants throughout the day. They talk to, play with, show affection to, and transmit subsistence skills to their infants during the day. I was rather surprised to find parents teaching their eight-to-twelve-month-old infants how to use small pointed digging sticks, throw small spears, use miniature axes with sharp metal blades, and carry small baskets. Most of this direct teaching takes place while resting on the net hunt. Unlike their village neighbors, Aka infants are carried in a sling on the side rather than on the back, which allows for more face-to-face interaction with the caregiver.

The Aka identify two stages within infancy—*molope,* from the time of birth until the infant can crawl, and *dibinda,* from the time of crawling and eating of solid foods until the child walks, at which time the infant is called *mona.* The term *mona* can be used up to seven to eight years of age. Unlike the !Kung hunter-gatherers (Konner 1976) Aka do not believe that infants have to be directly trained to walk or crawl. Like the !Kung, though, Aka infants receive plenty of vestibular stimulation as they are carried vertically most of the day. Infants will sleep for hours in the sling as parents set up nets and chase after game. The increased vestibular stimulation may contribute to the Aka infants' precocious motor and cognitive development described by Neuwelt-Truntzer (1981). Aka infants are smaller than American infants, but this does not appear to be a result of malnutrition. A study of infant health and nutrition (Cordes and Hewlett 1990) and Neuwelt-Truntzer's developmental tests indicate that Aka infants are healthy, especially by comparison to infants in other parts of the Third World, and that their motor and cognitive development is normal for their age.

While Aka are very indulgent and intimate with their infants, they are not a child-focused society. Some have suggested that many American parents are child-focused, in that parents will give undivided attention to the child (quality time) and dramatically change their behavior or activities to attend to the desires of their children. American parents allow their children to interrupt their conversations with other adults; they ask their children what they want to eat and try to accommodate other desires of the children. Aka society is adult-centered in that parents seldom stop their activities to pay undivided attention to their children. If an infant fusses or urinates on a parent who is talking to others or playing the drums, the parent continues his activity while gently rocking the infant or wiping the urine off with a nearby leaf. There are times when the infant's desires are not considered and the infant is actually placed in danger by the parents. For instance, on the net hunt, if a woman

33

chases a game animal into the net, she will place the infant on the ground to run after the game and kill it. The infant is left there crying until the mother or someone else comes back.

While mother is the primary and father the secondary caregiver, numerous others help out with infant care. While in the camp setting, Aka one-to-four-month-old infants are held by their mothers less than 40 percent of the time, are transferred to other caregivers an average of 7.3 times per hour, and have seven different caregivers on average that hold the infant during the day. The multiple caregiving decreases as the group moves out of camp to travel or go net hunting. Outside of camp, the mother holds the infant almost 90 percent of the time and the infant is transferred only two times per hour on average (Hewlett 1989a).

Unlike their farming neighbors and many other farming communities (Weisner and Gallimore 1977), older Aka infants are not placed under the care of an older, usually female, sibling on a regular basis. Older siblings may help periodically, but often it is because they want to care for the infant, not because they are given the infant to care for by the mother or are given the responsibility. Generally, it is difficult for parents to get their older children to do much for them at all. Older children (seven to eleven year olds) are asked to collect water or firewood but often simply ignore their parents' requests. The parents may yell at their children, but more often than not, they just go and get what they need by themselves. Children are independent and autonomous at an early age. The training for autonomy begins in infancy. Infants are allowed to crawl or walk to wherever they want in camp and allowed to use knives, machetes, digging sticks, and clay pots around camp. Only if an infant begins to crawl into a fire or hits another child do parents or others interfere with the infant's activity. It was not unusual, for instance, to see an eight month old with a six-inch knife chopping the branch frame of its family's house. By three or four years of age children can cook themselves a meal on the fire, and by ten years of age Aka children know enough subsistence skills to live in the forest alone if need be (Hewlett and Cavalli-Sforza 1986). Respect for an individual's autonomy is a core value among the Aka, and it is demonstrated and encouraged in their patterns of infant care.

The great respect for autonomy is consistent with another Aka value—intergenerational equality. This is a positive description of what villagers would call a lack of respect for elders. On one occasion a group of three young children (one to four year olds) was left in camp with an elderly man and an adult woman. During the day the kids started to tease and throw sticks at the elderly man. He tried to get them to stop but they continued to come back. The adult woman was not within view of the children. Eventually the old man just got up and walked into the forest and stayed there for three days. The Aka never got after the children for doing this. One villager in camp at the time chastised the Aka adults for not being more strict with their children and teaching them to respect their elders. Unlike their village neighbors, Aka infants and children are not socialized to be respectful, deferent, and obedient to elders. As mentioned, Aka infants can interfere with adult activities and not get punished.

Besides being indulgent and intimate, Aka infancy also lacks negation and violence, which are relatively common in American infancy. Seldom does one hear a parent tell an infant not to touch this or that or not to do something. As already mentioned if an infant hits another child a parent will get up and move the infant to another area; the infant is not told *no no*! Violence or corporal punishment for an infant that misbehaves seldom occurs. In fact, if one parent hits an infant, this is reason enough for the other parent to ask for a divorce.

While fathers are very active in infant care, they do not participate in the birth of their infants. Usually only women and young children attend births. One father I met attended and helped in the delivery of his infant but only because his wife gave birth while they were walking together in the forest. He was not teased or stigmatized for his participation. Both mother and father observe food taboos during the pregnancy and until the infant can walk well. There is also a postpartum sex taboo until the child can walk very

35

well. If one eats a taboo food or has marital or extramarital sex during the first year or two, the infant and/or the parents can get sick and possibly die. *Ekila,* an illness in which the infant goes into convulsions, is caused by the parents eating a taboo food and is the second leading cause of death among infants (Hewlett, van de Koppel, and van de Koppel 1986). Most Aka know about the postpartum sex taboo, but limited interview data and impressions indicate it is not observed. Even if one does break the rule there are indigenous medications to remedy the transgression.

In summary, Aka infancy has the following characteristics: constant holding and skin-to-skin contact, high father involvement, multiple caregiving, indulgent care, lack of negation, early training for autonomy and subsistence skills, parents as primary transmitters of culture, and precocious motor and cognitive development.

Childhood

Since infancy is to the topic of this study, only a limited description of childhood will be provided.

Weaning usually begins at age three or four when the mother becomes pregnant again. This relatively short developmental stage is called *djosi*. Once the newborn arrives, changes occur in the child's daily activities. The child, now called *mona,* is not able to walk fast enough to keep up with the net hunt and it is difficult for parents to transport two children on the hunt (i.e., the newborn and young child), so the four to five year old frequently stays behind in camp with one or two other children and an adult. The other children may be the same age or may be older children who did not want to go on the hunt. The children play, explore and practice subsistence skills and seldom venture more than fifty meters from camp. There is no special children's play area as described by Turnbull (1965b) for the Mbuti. The adult that stays behind does not watch them closely or instruct them in any skills but is always within earshot if help is necessary. In camp, before and after the hunt, most of the child's interaction and activities occur in and around the nuclear family hut.

When children can keep up with the net hunt (about age seven or eight), they join their parents on the hunt. Boys at this developmental stage are called *mona bokala* and girls are called *mona ngondo*. A boy tends to stay close to his father and a girl close to her mother, but the child makes the decision whom to follow and will usually follow the parent of the opposite sex for at least part of the day. Mothers and fathers are likely to ask for (but may not receive) the assistance of their son or daughter. The assisting son or daughter will receive more specific knowledge of subsistence techniques from the parent. Instruction is still primarily by observation and imitation, but verbal instructions are also given. At times during the net hunt, groups of children get together and play, but eventually they break up and return to the location of their parent's net. In camp the majority of the child's time is spent within a multiage play group, but always in the company of adults; the child's activity is no longer centered around the parental hut. If children have living grandparents in camp, they often sleep and eat with them.

By age eleven or twelve, same-sex and similar-age groups are quite distinct. At this developmental stage boys are called *bokala* and girls *ngondo*. Younger children have a tendency to play in same-sex, multiage groups, but by adolescence the few same-sex peers seem to be inseparable. While their activities are not totally independent of their parents (they often sleep and eat with their parents and stay near them on the net hunt), adolescents spend most of their time with same-sex peers. Girls of this age collect water, nuts, or fruit together, while boys take trips to the village or go on small game hunts together. The size of the same-sex group depends on the size, age, and sex distribution of the camp, but it often consists of three to four same-sex twelve to eighteen year olds. This is also a time of travel to visit relatives and explore territories other than the one they grew up in, so adolescents may be absent from the camp for long periods.

GENDER RELATIONS

Aka male-female relations are extremely egalitarian by cross-cultural standards. There is little agreement on how to determine gender equality/inequality (Mukhopadhay and Higgins 1988), but in all domains that are consistently mentioned in the literature, the Aka fall on the egalitarian side. Four domains of male-female relations will be considered here: economic, autonomy, power and prestige, and health and nutrition. Since this study concerns parenting, an emphasis will be placed upon the husband-wife relationship.

Women and men have considerable equality in the economic domain. While systematic studies on the caloric contributions of males versus females have not been conducted, it is clear that both males and females are regular contributors to the diet. What is especially remarkable about the Aka is the amount of time husband and wife spend in cooperative subsistence activity. Husband and wife are together on a regular basis to net hunt, collect caterpillars, termites, honey, fruit, and sometimes fish. On net hunting days husband and wife are within view of each other 47 percent of the time (Hewlett 1989b). They are not only in association with each other but actively cooperating in subsistence activity. On days when there is no net hunt, it is not unusual to see a husband and wife going out together to collect plants or honey (see pl. 5). Wives are less likely to participate in crossbow hunting for monkeys and trapline hunting for medium size game and never participate in spear hunts for wild pig and elephants. Aka husbands and wives are together often and cooperate in a wide variety of subsistence tasks throughout the year; they clearly care for one another, but it is also clear that Aka men and women like to be with members of the same sex at least as much as being with their spouses. Men enjoy hunting game together, and women enjoy collecting nuts and fruit away from the men.

Although not based upon systematic measures, men contribute slightly more to the diet while in the forest camps because in addition to the net hunting, men hunt for monkeys, pigs, and elephants, and collect most of the honey. In the village camps females are the primary providers, contributing at least 70 percent of the calories. While in the village, Aka women work in the fields of Ngandu women and receive manioc, corn, and palm oil in exchange for their labor. Similar to village men, Aka men do very little in the village camps. They may cut down palm nut regimes or clear coffee fields for villagers. Men spend about 10 percent of their day in productive labor in the village, in comparison to 60 percent in the forest (see chap. 4 for more details). When the camp is close to the village the Aka are more likely to follow the village pattern of separate gender subsistence activities. Approximately three to four months of the year are spent in the village.

Women not only contribute substantially to the diet but have considerable control over the distribution and exchange of food. Both women and men butcher and distribute game captured on the net hunt, and if it has been a reasonably good hunt women will prepare pots of food for other camp households. Sharing among the Aka is essentially a two-tier process. First, game is divided by the owners of the net (husband and wife) according to who jumped on the animal, who killed the the animal, and who helped set up the net. Once this division has taken place the game is taken back to camp and cooked. It is then distributed again by the woman that prepares the food. Women also distribute gathered food—mushrooms, fruit, nuts, tubers. A woman may distribute gathered food out in the forest, when she returns to camp or after she has prepared the food. Animals captured with other hunting techniques—monkeys, pigs, elephants, or gorillas—are divided by the individual who killed the animal. Patterns of sharing vary with the species of game (Bahuchet 1985). Besides having a central role in the distribution of food, women are primarily responsible for exchange with villagers. Villagers provide manioc, corn, salt, and other village goods in exchange for the Aka meat, *koko*, and other forest products. While deep in the forest, Aka and Ngandu women meet at a predetermined place halfway between the village and forest camp in order to exchange items. Since the baskets are heavy for these trading expeditions, the

39

women in camp may be gone for two or three days. But when Aka-Ngandu exchange occurs in the camp, it is usually the Aka women who exchange goods, regardless of the villager's gender.

The political power and social prestige of Aka women are pronounced but are not as structurally salient as those of Aka men. Aka men hold all the named positions of status—*kombeti, tuma,* and *nganga*—but as mentioned already, these men hold no absolute power. They influence people through their hospitality, persuasiveness, humor, and knowledge, not by their position. Aka women challenge men's authority on a regular basis and are influential actors in all kinds of decision making. Women participate in decisions about camp movement, extramarital affairs, bad luck on the hunt, and sorcery accusations. There is something of a matriarchy in many camps as the mother of the men who form the core of the camp is often the eldest patriclan member. Since men marry younger women, Aka women usually outlive their husbands by many years. These grandmothers eventually move back to the camp of their patriclan. Women in this position are vivacious characters and become respected patriclan spokespersons. The men in the named status positions are usually their sons. In terms of prestige, women's lines, *mobila,* are recognized and origin myths have men and women originating from a female fruit. Women have their own dances and songs in which they ridicule men. Kisliuk (1990) reports the lyrics for one *dingboku* (woman's dance) song: "the penis is not a competitor, it has died already! the vagina wins!" McCreedy (1990) describes the importance of women in Aka ritual life, especially the net hunt *bobanda* ritual. While there are many rituals and dances that clearly demonstrate the power and prestige of women, most rituals and dances involve both men and women in their separate but respected and complementary roles.

Autonomy within the context of group interdependence is a vital feature of Aka gender relations. Husbands and wives cooperate in a wide range of activities, but there is respect for each other's feelings and peculiarities. Husbands cannot force their wives to come on the hunt, and wives cannot force their husbands to look for honey. Spouses can and do ridicule each other with rather crude joking (e.g., uncomplimentary remarks about the size and shape of the partner's genitals), but for the most part the partner does not pay much attention to the ridicule. If the couple does not get along, divorce is a matter of one partner simply moving out of the house. While men and women have clearly defined subsistence and social roles, one is not ridiculed for trying a role usually assigned to the other gender. Women carry the nets, spears, and crossbows of the men, and men carry the baskets and digging sticks of the women. This sex role flexibility is seen in the different types of net hunt. On most net hunts, men go to the center of the nets and chase the game into the nets while women stand nearby to jump on and kill the captured game. But for social or environmental reasons (getting tired of doing one type of net hunt or trying to capture especially large game), the roles are sometimes reversed, and women go to the center of the nets while men stay next to the nets.

Physical violence in general is infrequent and violence against women is especially rare. The lack of violence enhances female autonomy and encourages husband-wife cooperation and trust. It is rather remarkable that after working on and off for fifteen years with the Aka I have yet to witness a violent act against a woman. I have asked colleagues who have spent considerable time with Aka, and they are also unable to report a case of violence against a woman. Husband-wife conflicts do of course occur but they are usually resolved through talking, rough joking, leaving camp for a while, or mediated assistance from other camp members. I have witnessed female violence against men. Women have cut their husbands' faces with knives and have hit their husbands with logs from the fire for sleeping with other women. Women, however, are more likely to show their anger and displeasure with their husbands by tearing down the family house. Aka women make the houses, and Aka men are not very good at it (they usually make lean-tos). Female autonomy and the lack of violence against women are also demonstrated by the frequent travel of women, alone or in small groups, throughout the forest.

41

Recent studies of Aka health and nutrition (Cordes and Hewlett 1990; Walker and Hewlett 1990) provide objective indicators of both gender equality and inequality. Aka females under five appear to have slightly better health and nutrition than Aka males of the same age, while Aka males are more likely to have better health and nutrition in adulthood. Aka females under five have significantly higher hemoglobins than Aka males of the same age. The young females also have slightly larger arm circumferences and skin folds than the young boys. The differences disappear by age ten, and by adulthood the pattern partially reverses itself, the adult males having significantly higher hemoglobins than adult females. Adult females do continue to have larger skin folds and arm circumferences than the males. Adult males also have better dental health than adult females; the adult males had fewer dental caries and missing teeth than the adult females. The nutritional demands of lactation may explain the prevalence of high tooth loss, but the higher caries rate is related to a diet higher in carbohydrates and lower in protein and fats than that of adult men. A male diet higher in protein is also suggested by the hemoglobin data. Finally, Aka mortality data indicate that, unlike the Ache, Batek, and Inuit hunter-gatherers where statistically more males survive to adulthood than females, there is no preferential treatment of boys over girls. While there are differences in the health of Aka adult men and women, there are numerous similarities: both men and women have similar blood pressure throughout the lifespan, they have essentially the same prevalence of splenomegaly and hepatomegaly, and they have similar height-to-weight ratios.

It is essential to understand Aka gender relations, particularly husband-wife relations, if one is to understand the Aka father-infant relationship. Husband and wife are together often, know each other exceptionally well, and cooperate on a regular basis in a diversity of tasks. Men and women have distinct tasks, but there are few underlying beliefs that one sex is naturally inclined to perform certain tasks. The capabilities of men and women are very similar, and therefore tasks can be reversed easily. Male and female experiences and socialization are different, but men and women know the tasks of the opposite sex. Women are also valued and respected members of the group. Aka men, however, are similar to men cross-culturally in that men predominate in the named status positions, only men hunt large game, and polygyny is relatively common. In summary, Aka male-female relations have commonalties with male-female relations cross-culturally, but the Aka are probably as egalitarian as human societies get.

THE VILLAGE WORLD—THE AKA SOCIAL ENVIRONMENT

It is impossible to provide a holistic view of Aka life without describing the Ngandu farmers with whom the Aka have a semisymbiotic trading relationship. Aka throughout the CAR and PRC have trading relationships with at least fifteen ethnically and linguistically distinct farming-hunting-fishing populations. The Ngandu speak a Bantu language totally different from the Bantu of the Aka and moved into the area only 120 years ago.

Turnbull's characterization of distinct forest and village worlds (1965a, 1965b) does not apply to the Ngandu and Aka. Ngandu men and women go into the forest on a regular basis and the Aka depend heavily on Ngandu for manioc and other village goods. But Turnbull's ethnographies do capture the distinctive ambiance of the village and forest worlds. In this brief section I will not try to duplicate Turnbull's exceptional work but will simply identify some contrasting features of Aka and Ngandu cultures.

The Ngandu farm manioc, plantain, yams, taro, maize, cucumbers, squash, okra, papaya, mango, pineapple, palm oil, and rice. The domesticated crops provide the majority of calories to their diet during the year. They also keep chickens, muskovy ducks, goats, sheep, and dogs. Men hunt occasionally with crossbows, steel-wire snares, and guns for monkeys, a variety of small duikers, wild pigs, bongos and other mammals. All Ngandu grow at least some coffee as a cash crop. Ngandu men occasionally hunt, but they receive the majority of their meat through trade with the Aka. The Aka provide the Ngandu with game meat, honey, *koko,* and other forest products, and the Ngandu provide the Aka with manioc and other village products. There are a government-supported school, dispensary, and police station in the village.

Ngandu women are the primary contributors to the diet but have substantially lower status than Aka women. Violence against women and children exists, and women seldom participate in political decision making. Men spend little time in subsistence activities and spend their time politicking, talking, and drinking palm wine with other men. Polygyny is about 45 percent, and fertility is slightly lower due to a greater prevalence of STDs (sexually transmitted diseases) and consequent female infertility. Ngandu often remark about the exceptional fertility of Aka women, but only occasionally does an Ngandu man marry an Aka woman. Ngandu women never marry Aka men. Child mortality may be slightly lower among the Ngandu because the government nurse periodically provides childhood immunizations, antimalarial drugs, aspirin, and oral rehydration mix.

The kinship and marriage patterns are quite distinct. The Ngandu males live in the same house and village most of their adult life and have strong localized patriclans. The patriclan is a social support network and is a major force in determining who helps whom in village disputes and in organizing ritual activities, especially funerals. The Ngandu do share food with clan and family members and hospitality is an important cultural value, but it is relatively infrequent in comparison with the daily sharing among the Aka. Ngandu males provide bride wealth rather than bride service to obtain a spouse, which means there is no temporary matrilocality among the Ngandu. If there is a divorce, the children belong to the patriclan and will usually stay with the father's family. Among the Aka, children decide with their parents whom they will live with. Ngandu and Aka infants always stay with mother.

Ngandu draw attention to themselves whenever possible. If they have killed a monkey with a gun, have a new machete, or a new blouse, they visit people to show off the item. This contrasts with the Aka pattern of prestige avoidance. Ngandu are also accumulators and material wealth increases both an individual's and clan's prestige. Aka seldom asked me for clothes or other material items while Ngandu were persistent and assertive in their demands for items.

There is greater standardization in Ngandu religious life. Beliefs in sorcery predominate Ngandu life, and it is not uncommon for an individual to be in the custody of the mayor or the police for practicing sorcery. Most illness and death are attributed to sorcery. Ancestor spirits are also important and can assist or cause harm to family members. Most Ngandu have had some exposure to Western religions. There are a Catholic and a Baha'i church in the village and Protestant missionaries make regular visits. A number of missionaries have tried to work with the Aka but none have succeeded in maintaining contact because the Aka move camp so often.

The Ngandu generally see themselves as the owners of the Aka. The Ngandu and their trading partners have the same clan name. Aka are expected to provide occasional gifts of meat, honey, or caterpillars to their *konza* (patron). When an Aka baby is born the Ngandu trading partner of the family is delighted because the baby represents another worker. Some Ngandu are relatively egalitarian in their relationship with Aka, while others are extremely exploitive. I have witnessed four instances of villagers beating an Aka because the person disobeyed, stole from, or cheated the villager.

Health and disease patterns are somewhat different. Ngandu have more bronchitis and respiratory problems, a higher prevalence of STDs, higher blood pressure, and a higher prevalence of goiter. The Aka have lower hemoglobins and a higher prevalence of yaws, splenomegaly, hepatomegaly, and tropical ulcers.

Socialization practices are extremely different in the two populations. Ngandu fathers provide a minimal amount of direct care to infants and children; mothers and older female siblings are the primary caregivers. There is no multiple care as described for the Aka; Ngandu infant care may be called "polymatric" in that the mother

45

usually gets assistance from an older female sibling or one or two other female relatives. Children are socialized to be obedient and respectful and can receive corporal punishment if they do not heed their parents' requests. I asked Aka parents what things they liked most and least about Ngandu child-rearing patterns. Aka parents did not like how often the Ngandu beat their children, but they did like how the Ngandu children listened to their parents!

Ngandu children have same-sex, similar age playmates early on because the village is much larger than the Aka camp. Cultural transmission is more horizontal (friends and peers-to-child) than vertical (parent-to-child) due to the different physical settings. Older children, especially girls, are expected to make regular contributions to subsistence and domestic activities (e.g., getting firewood or water and helping in the fields), whereas Aka children are not expected to contribute to subsistence until early adulthood, usually when they get married. Ngandu children learn to be deferent to elders, teachers, and village chiefs, whereas Aka children do not learn or practice deference toward Aka elders, the *kombeti,* or the *tuma*.

Village life and forest life are very different. In the forest the Aka are lively and playful during the day; dancing and singing occur most evenings. Autonomy, cooperation, and play characterize forest life. Village life is lively and social and long visits with neighbors occur throughout the day, but village life is more cautious and restrained. It is important to be sensitive to the needs of others and demonstrate deference and respect to many people—older brothers, parents, government officials, older male clan members, and the elderly.

This overview provides the backdrop for understanding the nature of the Aka father-infant relationship. The next three chapters link the various cultural components described in this chapter to various facets of the father-infant relationship. The following chapter outlines the methods used in the father-infant study.

CHAPTER 3

Methods

This chapter describes in detail the various methods used in the father-infant study. The chapter actually lists each type of behavior coded and the questions asked in interviews. In many studies the methodological details are placed in an appendix at the end of the book. Appendixes are seldom read unless the reader is highly motivated or has a vested interest in the material. Since methods are central to understanding the implications and limitations of a study, they are detailed in this chapter. The chapter aims to give the reader a clear picture of what actually happened (and did not happen) while in the field, rather than simply stating that the standard anthropological methodology—participant observation—was used. It is not necessary to read this chapter as closely as the others. It is intended to provide the opportunity to understand and scrutinize the various field methods.

PREVIOUS FIELD STUDIES OF SOCIALIZATION AMONG AFRICAN PYGMIES

Previous socialization studies of African Pygmies influenced the design of this father-infant study. Turnbull's ethnographies (1961, 1965b) and socialization studies (1978, 1981) were influential in a number of respects. First, in his ethnographic survey of the Ituri Pygmies, Turnbull indicates that net hunting fathers are more involved with children than are archer fathers:

It (bow hunting) is not essentially cooperative, and it does not include women and children, so placing the sexes in different relationships with the forest . . . There is not only greater parity between the sexes among the net hunters, but also the father enters more fully into family life than among the archers. (1965a:262)

Second, Turnbull suggests few differences between mother and father in the style of caregiving; "If anything, the father is just another kind of mother" (1983:41). Third, Turnbull emphasizes the communal socialization of the children. He describes what an Mbuti adult would do if an infant crawled into the ashes of a fire hearth:

In a moment he will be surrounded by angry adults and given a sound slapping, then carried unceremoniously back to the safety of a hut. It does not matter which hut, because as far as the child is concerned all adults are his parents or grandparents. They are all equally likely to slap him for doing wrong, fondle him and feed him with delicacies, if he is quiet and gives no trouble. He knows his real mother and father, of course, and has special affection for them and they for him, but from an early age he learns that he is the child of them all, for they are all children of the forest. (1961:127)

Turnbull influenced this study in that before going into the field to quantitatively investigate Aka fathers, his qualitative descriptions of indulgent fathers among Mbuti net hunters matched my own earlier nonsystematic observations of Aka net hunters. His observations encouraged my study of Aka fathers. While our observations were similar on the first point, my own informal observations of Aka did not fit well with Turnbull's on the last two points—not all adults are the Aka child's parents and Aka seldom, if ever, slap their children. Chapters four and five present data that support Turnbull's first point but contradict the second and third points.

48

This research was also influenced by members of a major longitudinal multidisciplinary study of the Efe Pygmies (the archers) and Lese farmers of the northern part of the Ituri Forest in Zaire directed by Irven DeVore and Robert Bailey (Bailey 1985). Before going into the field, I had discussions with many members of the project, but conversations with Edward Tronick and Gilda Morelli, who were responsible for the child development component of the research, were especially instructive. Their preliminary work suggested that Efe fathers did very little caretaking. Given their experience with Efe, they seriously doubted that Aka fathers were doing as much caregiving as I described from informal observations. They emphasized the importance of quantification and comparability of behavioral codes, and as a consequence many of the codes that were used in this study were derived from conversations with and data provided by members of the Ituri Project.

Finally, two psychologically oriented studies conducted among the Aka Pygmies influenced this study of father-infant relations. The first study was under the direction of Herman Witkin and John Berry. Psychologists spent three six-month periods between 1975 and 1977 investigating "field dependence and independence" among the Aka Pygmies and Ngandu farmers of the Central African Republic. Field independence means that one's actions and perceptions are generally seen as separate from others, whereas field dependence means that one's self and perceptions are embedded within a larger framework. Psychological tests indicated that the Aka were field independent (once one controlled for acculturation) while the Ngandu were field dependent (van de Koppel 1983). The researchers indicated that socialization practices generated these different patterns; Aka parents encouraged autonomy, did not employ severe discipline methods to control their children, and did not stress conformity of their children. The Ngandu farmers on the other hand had just the opposite socialization practices. While an interesting study of socialization, one does not get a clear idea of the specific child-rearing methods by which Aka autonomy and personal responsibility are encouraged. The lack of specific data on socialization practices was due in part to the emphasis on the administration of psychological tests to Aka and Ngandu in a village laboratory. Few members of the team ever lived in the forest with the Aka. Their research, however, did provide a general outline of Aka socialization practices before I began the father-infant study. In regard to fathers, van de Koppel mentions that fathers were often seen caring for babies (1983:21).

The other Aka "psychological" study was conducted by Neuwelt-Truntzer (1981) under the direction of Robert LeVine. She went into the field to test LeVine's hypothesis that societies with high infant mortality should have child-rearing techniques and parental goals that reflect a concern for the infant's survival. In societies with high infant mortality, LeVine predicted that the infant would be held most of the time, fed on demand, and that crying would be responded to quickly. Neuwelt-Truntzer found support for LeVine's hypothesis among the Aka, as infant mortality was high (22 percent) and child-rearing techniques had the aforementioned characteristics. Neuwelt-Truntzer's study provided useful data for the father-infant study. First, she measured Aka motor and cognitive development with standardized tests (Bailey Developmental and Uzgiris-Hunt Developmental Test) and found the Aka to be mildly precocious in comparison with other human populations. Since she had conducted the developmental testing of Aka infants, I felt that it was unnecessary to replicate the time-consuming developmental tests in the father-infant study. She demonstrated that Aka infants develop within a normal range. These are critical data because once a comparison is made between the Aka father-infant relationship and the father-infant relationship in another culture, one has to know whether the infants in both cultures have "normal" motor and cognitive development. Second, she did conduct behavioral observations, but only between the hours of 8:00 A.M. and 2:00 P.M., and only in the camp setting. Some of her behavioral codes were used in this study, but after talking with members of the Ituri Project I decided to attempt all-day focal observations.

BEHAVIORAL OBSERVATIONS

Anthropologists who have attempted to quantify human behavior have generally used spot or scan sampling techniques (Erasmus 1955; Munroe and Munroe 1971; Whiting and Whiting 1975; Johnson 1975; Hames 1978; Borgerhoff Mulder and Caro 1985). With this method the activities and states of all the individuals within view at one location and at one point in time are recorded. It is a very efficient and relatively easy way to quantify the activities of a large number of individuals in a given population. The number of random scans or spot observations conducted during a study period has varied from a few hundred (Johnson 1975) to over a hundred thousand (Hames 1978). The aim of this technique is to measure types of human activity; it is not very useful for measuring the style or nature of human interaction. A constraint of this technique is that individuals must be in accessible and predictable locations. If observations are to occur randomly throughout the day, the observer must be able to locate individuals relatively easily. Consequently, spot and scan sampling techniques have been utilized extensively in sedentary farming populations where individuals can usually be located in the village or in nearby village fields.

Spot or scan sampling did not seem appropriate in this investigation of Aka Pygmy father-infant interaction because Aka Pygmies are very mobile, the location of daily activities is very unpredictable, and the project aimed at quantifying style as well as frequency of interaction. A focal subject observational technique seemed to be a much more efficient and applicable method. With this method, one individual is followed for a considerable amount of time, in this study, all day. Since one individual is followed all day, the style of interaction (type of play with infant, infant responses to caretaker) between the focal subject and other individuals as well as the general activities of the focal subject could be quantified.

All-Day Behavioral Observations

Three types of focal sampling (Altman 1974, 1980) were used: father focal all day (6 A.M. to 6 P.M.), infant focal all day, and infant focal for two morning hours. Father focal observations were conducted with each of the fifteen fathers on randomly selected days. Every fifteen minutes the father's activity, the people he was interacting with, the people touching him, the people within 1 m, the nearest neighbor to him, his availability to his infant, and the location and activity of the mother were noted (table 5). Modifications of Johnson's (1975) time-allocation activity codes were used to code mothers' and fathers' activities. Any direct interaction between the father and his infant was noted minute by minute: what the father did with the infant (caretaking, playing, soothing, etc.), what other activities he engaged in when holding the infant, and the mother's activity while he held the infant (table 6). Conditions of receiving the infant and for terminating the interaction were also noted. A condition for beginning a father focal observation was that the mother had to reside in the camp; she need not be present but she had to be living in the same camp as the father. Occasionally it was difficult or overly intrusive to keep the father within view (especially on a net hunt); consequently, observations were suspended during this time. The mean length of the fifteen father observations was 689.5 minutes (about 11.5 hours).

Father focal observations have not been conducted in previous cross-cultural child development studies for the simple reason that fathers usually have infrequent contact with children; father focal observations would take considerable time and energy to gain relatively little data on father-infant relations. Consequently, infant and mother focal observational techniques have dominated previous studies. Father observations were attempted in this study because fathers were known to do considerable caretaking, and it was important to determine what fathers do while they are not spending time with their infants.

All-day infant focal observations were conducted with six infants

TABLE 5.   Items Coded Every Fifteen Minutes during Father Focal Observations

(1) Setting

    1 = forest camp
    2 = forest camp during dance
    3 = forest trail on way to or returning from net hunt
    4 = forest net hunt on rest (includes first fire)
    5 = forest net hunt—all other
    6 = forest—all other
    7 = village camp
    8 = village camp during dance
    9 = village trail in field
  10 = village fields to work for villager
  11 = village fields to look for palm wine
  12 = village center
  13 = village—all other
  14 = forest—before net hunt, looking for honey or fruit

(2) Position of Father

    1 = sleep
    2 = lie
    3 = sit
    4 = walk
    5 = dance
    6 = climb
    7 = not visible
    8 = other
    9 = squat
  10 = stand
  11 = run
  12 = no data

(3) Primary activity

    1 = eating (includes snacks)
    2 = food preparation (includes water and firewood collection)
    3 = child care (nursing, holding, playing, cleaning)
    4 = manufacture (spear, axe, kusa, hut, etc.)
    5 = hunting (note: sitting next to net with infant is hunting)
    6 = collecting (includes collecting leaves for hut)
    7 = idle (doing nothing, sleeping, talking, resting on hunt)
    8 = hygiene (going toilet, cleaning pots, washing)

(*continued*)

TABLE 5—*Continued*

9 = visiting (includes visiting others in same camp)
11 = garden labor (for villager)
12 = no data
13 = exchanging with villager
14 = other—looking for missing people
15 = dancing

(4) Items carried (code only when person walking or standing)

0 = nothing carried
1 = net
2 = spear
3 = axe
4 = basket
5 = digging stick
6 = infant
7 = net and spear
8 = net and axe
9 = net, spear, and axe
10 = basket and digging stick
11 = basket, digging stick, and infant
12 = no data
13 = infant and basket
14 = firewood (on shoulder only)
15 = other—e.g., meat in hands
16 = spear and axe
17 = two children (infant and young child)

(5) Vocalization

0 = none
1 = talking with/to someone
2 = singing
3 = yelling to scare animals
4 = vocalizing to give location (ya, yo, etc.)
5 = singing to give location
12 = no data

(6) Identification of person speaking to/with

1 = wife or husband
2 = focal infant

TABLE 5—*Continued*

3 = other male adults (on net hunt or in camp)
4 = other adults (on net hunt or in camp)
5 = villagers
12 = no data
    list all others by I.D. number

(7) Touching

1 = wife
2 = focal infant
3 = wife and focal infant
5 = no touching, no proximity, no nearest neighbor (besides hold)
12 = no data
    list all people touching by I.D. number

(8) Proximity

list all people within one meter

(9) Nearest neighbor (other than holding)

list I.D. number of closest person with ten meters (but not being held by subject)

(10) General activity with infant

1 = transporting (no interaction)
2 = playing (as primary activity only)
3 = nursing
4 = watching infant to help out mother
5 = no interaction, infant nearby, but more than 1 m away
6 = feeding
7 = no interaction, infant just being held or sitting on lap (includes sleeping)
8 = other caretaking—e.g., putting on protective cord
10 = talking with
11 = no interaction, infant playing alone less than 1 m away
12 = no data
13 = soothing, singing to
14 = cleaning, washing, delicing

(*continued*)

TABLE 5—*Continued*

(11) Position of mother (if within view) (same codes as 2 above)/Items carried (same as 4 above)

(12) General Activity—A) Of mother; B) With infant

two codes should be listed in this box—on the left hand of the bar should be a code from (3) above, and on the right hand of the bar should be a code from (10) above

(13) Location of infant (if within view) in camp (forest or village)

    1 = in family hut
    2 = near (approx. 1 m) family hut
    3 = in or around nonnuclear family hut
    4 = with natural parent(s)
    5 = under care by nonparent
    6 = in or around grandparents' hut
    7 = just outside camp (within sight) in forest or village fields
    12 = no data

(14) Activity of infant

    1 = nursing
    2 = idle (just sitting or being held)
    3 = sleeping
    4 = eating
    5 = visiting
    6 = subsistence play—alone
    7 = subsistence play—with other children
    8 = playing with other children (object and social play)
    9 = playing/exploring alone
    10 = playing with object as sitting on lap or being held
    11 = talking/vocalizing with parent
    12 = no data
    13 = playing with adult(s)
    14 = fussing
    15 = being cleaned by adult

(15) Infant held by

    1 = mother
    2 = father

TABLE 5—*Continued*

12 = no data
    if not mother or father list I.D. number

(16) Infant being touched by/Infant within proximity of

proximity measure should include all individuals within 1 m

(17) Availability of mother and father (always two codes in #17)

    1 = within visual range of mother
    2 = within hearing range of mother (if infant were to cry or scream)
    3 = mother out of area/not available
    4 = within visual range of father
    5 = within hearing range of father
    6 = father out of area/not available
    12 = unable to determine/lack of data

TABLE 6.   Items Coded Continuously (Whenever They Occurred) during Father Focal and Infant Focal Observations

(1) Infant being held

    A. identification of caretaker
    B. time hold began and ended
    C. condition under which caretaker started hold
        1 = mother gives infant to father or vice versa
        2 = father takes infant from mother or vice versa
        3 = nonparent gives to mother or father
        4 = mother or father takes from nonparent
        5 = infant walks or crawls to person
        6 = infant fusses or cries for mother or father and nonparent caretaker
           takes to parent
        7 = caretaker picks infant off ground—fussing
        8 = caretaker picks infant off ground or bed—no fussing by infant
    D. condition under which hold ended
        1 = infant fusses for, reaches for, so caretaker gives to person infant
           shows attachment for
        2 = infant crawls or walks to another caretaker
        3 = another caretaker simply comes and takes infant—no fussing
        4 = caretaker gives to another person because infant fussing
        5 = one caretaker gives to another— no fussing
        6 = caretaker puts infant down to play alone

(*continued*)

TABLE 6—*Continued*

7 = infant walks or crawls away on own—no new caretaker
12 = no data
E. setting (see setting codes in table 5) during hold noted minute by minute
F. mother's primary activity (see activity codes in table 5) while father held infant
G. interactions between caretaker and infant (list each time activity occurs during hold)
1 = feeding
2 = bathe, wash
3 = pick off dirt
4 = de-lice
5 = de-chic
6 = clean after bowel movement
7 = clean after urine
8 = control (keeping infant away from dangers)
9 = playing
10 = soothing
11 = affection
12 = infant fusses
H. primary activities of caretaker while holding infant (see activity codes in table 5)
I. if caretaker purposely picked up infant, what was primary reason for picking up infant (infant not given to caretaker)?
1. caretaking—to feed, transport, clean
2. control/discipline—to take from danger
3. play
4. soothing
5. clear request by infant to be picked up
6. simple desire of caretaker to pick up
7. other

(2) Caretaker playing with infant

A. identification of caretaker
B. time of day and setting (see table 5 for setting codes)
C. proximal condition
1 = person playing with infant is holding or touching
2 = person plays with infant as another person holds but is within proximity
3 = person plays with infant as another person holds but is more than 1 m away
4 = infant not being held or touched, person playing with is within 1 m
D. type of play if face-to-face play
1 = proximal
2 = distal

TABLE 6—*Continued*

3 = verbal
4 = physical
5 = visual
6 = tactile
7 = verbal and proximal
8 = distal and verbal
9 = tactile and physical
10 = distal and tactile
11 = distal, physical, visual
12 = proximal, verbal, tactile
13 = distal, verbal, visual
14 = proximal, physical, tactile
15 = verbal, physical, tactile
16 = proximal and tactile
17 = proximal, verbal, visual
18 = distal and verbal

E. type of play other than face-to-face
1 = rough-and-tumble, chase, major physical
2 = minor physical (tickling or nibbling)
3 = object—coordinate
4 = object—parallel (person and child next to each other)
5 = object—stimulus (person to stimulate the infant + hold attention)
6 = object—tease (take food or object away)
7 = face-to-face (also code above)
8 = other

F. type of response from infant
1 = very negative
2 = negative
3 = neutral
4 = content
5 = mildly positive
6 = positive
7 = very positive

(3) Infant nursing bouts (infant focal only)

A. setting (see table 5 for setting codes)
B. length of bout by number of seconds if possible

(4) Infant attachment behaviors (infant focal only)

A. time behavior demonstrated
B. setting (see table 5 for setting codes)
C. attachment behavior viewed:

(*continued*)

TABLE 6—*Continued*

        1 = approaching (crawling, walking to) (from beyond proximity to
            within proximity)
        2 = seeking to be held
        3 = reaches (raises and moving hand in direction of person; occasionally
            involves touching but only coded when not terminated in touch)
        4 = fusses for (distress type vocalization)
        5 = touch
        6 = proffer
        7 = crawls in lap

(5) Items infant held

    A. time and setting coded
    B. items:
        1 = machete
        2 = small knife
        3 = large knife
        4 = city object (can, bottle, etc.)
        5 = necklace around caretakers neck
        6 = bowl
        7 = *kusa* (string)
        8 = *sawala* (male purse)
        9 = other

(6) Duration of sleep during observation period (infant focal observations only)
    recorded by minute

(7) Infant crying or fussing

    A. caretaker while fussing
    B. caretakers response to fuss
        1 = ignore
        2 = devote total attention to soothing infant
        3 = devote partial attention to soothing as continue to engage in other
            activity
        4 = nurse or feed infant
        5 = other
    C. length of fuss by minute
    D. resolution of fuss
        1 = caretaker soothes by means other than nursing
        2 = caretaker soothes by nursing
        3 = caretaker gives to another caretaker to soothe
        4 = infant stops fuss on own (crawls or walks away)

(two from each age-group) residing in forest camps. This limitation was due to the fact that in the forest the primary subsistence activity was the net hunt in which almost everyone participated. Following the infant while it was held by the mother was not a problem because other adult males were nearby. In the village, however, female activity outside the camp was often solitary or restricted to a few other females, so a male observer could be intrusive (if not threatening) to both males and females. For this reason, no all-day infant focal observations were made in the village. To help compensate for the fewer infant focal hours, two additional hours of infant focal observation were conducted in camp on each of the fifteen infants. During infant focal observations, activity of the infant, infant proximity to others, and availability of mother and father were coded every 15 minutes (table 7). Types of behaviors coded (regardless of time) included: number and length of nursing bouts, types of play with others, types of play alone, attachment behaviors (reaching for, crying for, crawling to, touching), quality of caretaking (intensive or perfunctory), caretaker exchanges, and conditions under which exchanges occurred (table 6). A condition for beginning an infant focal observation was that the mother and father be residing in the camp (but not necessarily present) at the time of the observation. The average length of the all-day infant focal observations was 648.5 minutes (about 10.5 hours), while the average length of the morning 2-hour infant focal observations was 115.9 minutes (about 1.9 hours).

All-day father and infant observations in the forest were undertaken only on days in which a net hunt was performed. Net hunts were almost daily during much of the study period. There were days when it rained and people rested or searched for fruit or honey. Due to the limited number of total observations possible during the short study period, it was decided to limit forest observations to days when a net hunt occurred.

In total, this study is based on 264 hours of focal observation: 172 hours focusing on fathers and 92 hours focusing on infants.

TABLE 7. Items Coded Every Fifteen Minutes during Infant Focal Observations

(1)   Setting (see table 5 for codes)

(2)   Infant's position

      1 = lie and sleep
      2 = lie and awake
      3 = sit (unsupported)
      4 = walk
      5 = dance
      6 = climb
      7 = crawl
      8 = other
      9 = squat
    10 = stand
    11 = run
    12 = no data
    13 = being held on side of caretaker
    14 = being held on back of caretaker
    15 = sitting on lap of caretaker—supported or unsupported

(3)   Infant's location

      1 = in family hut
      2 = near family hut (within 2 m)
      3 = in or around nonnuclear family hut
      6 = in or around grandparents' hut
      7 = just outside camp (within sight)
            outside of camp
      4 = with natural parent(s)
      5 = under care of nonparent
    12 = no data

(4)   Infant's activity

      1 = sleeping
      2 = nursing
      3 = eating
      4 = playing
      5 = visiting (out of area of own hut)
      6 = in transit (being carried or passed to)
      7 = crying or fussing
      8 = idle—no activity
      9 = watching parent do something (but not being held)
    10 = doing task asked by parent
    12 = no activity

TABLE 7—*Continued*

(5) Held by

   1 = mother
   2 = father
   5 = not being held
   12 = no data
         list all others by I.D. number

(6) Touched by (codes same as held by)

(7) All individuals within proximity (1 m) of infant
     (not touching or holding) (same codes as held by)

(8) All individuals within 3 m of infant
     (not holding, touching or within proximity)
     (same codes as held by)

(9) All individuals within 5 m of infant
     (do not list those also within 3 m)
     (same codes as held by)

(10) Mother's position/items carried
      (see table 5 for codes)

(11) Mother's activity
      (see table 5 for codes)

(12) Father's position/items carried
      (see table 5 for codes)

(13) Father's activity
      (see table 5 for codes)

(14) Mother's availability
      (see table 5 for codes)

(15) Father's availability
      (see table 5 for codes)

Spot Observations

Spot observations were used on a limited basis. Once the sun went down (shortly after 6:30 P.M.), focal subject observations became uncomfortable for both observer and subject as the researcher had to sit extremely close in order to view interactions. As a consequence, spot observations were made with the fifteen sample families in order to get some idea of the amount of father-infant interaction in the evening hours. Spot observations were made from 6:30 P.M. until 9:00 P.M. regardless of whether the infant or parents were sleeping. Also, in order to check the observer's effect on all-day focal observations, occasional spot observations of mothers' and fathers' activities were made by the researcher and/or a trained research assistant. Reliability between researcher and research assistant's observations averaged .85 over the eight activity and availability items (table 8).

The Families

The sample consisted of fifteen Aka families with infants between one and eighteen months of age. Eight of the infants were female and seven were male, six between one and four months of age (two males, four females), five between eight and twelve months of age (three males, two females), and four between thirteen and eighteen months of age (two females, two males). Six families resided near the Ngandu village while observations were undertaken (two infants from each age category, one of each sex) while nine families lived in the forest (four infants in the one-to-four-month age category [three female, one male]), three infants in the eight-to-twelve-month category (two male, one female), and two infants in the last age category (one of each sex). Seven of the infants were firstborns to the couple (some from each age group), while eight of the families had other children (usually one other child). In three of the fifteen families, the father was polygynous (one father in each age group). Table 9 summarizes the characteristics of the sample.

TABLE 8.   Behaviors Examined during Spot Observations

(1) Position of infant (see table 7 for codes)

(2) Activity of infant (see table 7 for codes)

(3) Position of mother (see table 5 for codes)

(4) Activity of mother (see table 5 for codes)

(5) Availability of mother (see table 5 for codes)

(6) Position of father (see table 5 for codes)

(7) Activity of father (see table 5 for codes)

(8) Availability of father (see table 5 for codes)

TABLE 9.   Number and Types of Behavioral Observations

Infant Number	Observational Setting	Age Group (in months)	Sex	All Day Father Focal	All Day Infant Focal	2 Hour Infant Focal	P.M. Spot Observation
1	Forest	1–4	F	x	x	x	x
2	Forest	1–4	F	x	x	x	x
3	Village	1–4	F	x		x	x
4	Forest	1–4	M	x	x	x	x
5	Forest	1–4	M	x	x	x	x
6	Village	1–4	M	x		x	x
7	Forest	8–12	M	x	x	x	x
8	Village	8–12	M	x		x	x
9	Forest	8–12	M	x	x	x	x
10	Forest	8–12	F	x	x	x	x
11	Village	8–12	F	x		x	x
12	Forest	13–18	F	x	x	x	x
13	Forest	13–18	M	x	x	x	x
14	Village	13–18	M	x		x	x
15	Village	13–18	F	x		x	x

Specific rationale existed for selecting the three infant age groups mentioned above. One to four month olds were selected because U.S. studies have shown that differences exist between mothers' and fathers' play behavior even at this early stage (Parke and Sawin 1980). In face-to-face play, fathers were more proximal and physical (e.g., movement of limbs), whereas mothers provided more distal and verbal play. Eight to twelve month olds were included in the study because attachment theory (Bowlby 1969) states that attachment behaviors (crying for, reaching for particular others) emerge at this age, especially when the infant is threatened (by dangerous animals or unfamiliar individuals). It would be important to identify attachment behaviors expressed toward fathers, social-emotional setting of attachment behaviors demonstrated toward fathers, and differences between attachment behaviors toward fathers and mothers. Thirteen to eighteen month olds were selected for study because most Aka infants walk by this age. Increased mobility means the infant needs less direct caretaking (i.e., holding) and can at times select his or her caretaker. This developmental change has been shown to dramatically affect mothers' and fathers' childcare patterns (Chisholm 1983; Munroe and Munroe 1971). Also, since walking to a point within 1 m of another person is considered an attachment behavior by psychologists, it could provide a means of measuring distinctions in an infant's attachment behavior toward his or her mother and father.

The sample size was quite modest, especially in comparison with standards of Western psychological family observational studies. Since the mobile Aka live in small (twenty-five to thirty-five individuals), sparsely distributed camps it was necessary to travel 75 km on foot to establish this admittedly scant sample.

QUESTIONNAIRES

In order to elicit Aka conceptions and feelings about fathers, mothers, parenting and the father-infant/child relationship, and to see if expressed views reflected observed behavior, five structured questionnaires were administered. Sixteen women who recently gave birth were interviewed to ascertain such information as who assisted in the birth, complications, procedures, number and relationship of those present, father's role, length of time before lactation commenced, etc. (table 10). Sixteen eleven to fifteen year olds (eight boys, eight girls) were interviewed (table 11) to get a sense of their feelings toward and experiences with their mother and father (views toward stepparents were also included).

Two questionnaires were administered to two separate adult samples. Twenty adults (ten male, ten female) were interviewed about their childhood experiences and feelings toward their parents, and their expectations, experiences, and views toward their own children at various stages of development (see table 12 for list of questions). Another sample of twenty adults (ten male, ten female) was given a "responsibility" questionnaire. The purpose of these interviews was to get Aka conceptions of who does what infant care in their own family when certain caretakers are available or not available (table 13).

Finally, forty adults (twenty male, twenty female), sixteen adolescents (eight male, eight female), and sixteen children seven to eleven years old (eight boys, eight girls) were asked about who instructed them in fifty subsistence, maintenance, and childcare skills (table 14). An aim of these interviews was to determine whom Aka viewed as educators. Were mother and father contributors to skill knowledge, and if so what specific skills did they contribute?

All Aka interviewed came from the study area and were well known to me. An attempt was made to make the samples random, but often due to the small size of camps and daily changes in camp composition, the sample became more opportunistic. A random sample was selected to be interviewed, but if someone was not present I went to the next person on the list. Since the samples generally represent 25–50 percent of the total study population, almost everyone present in camp was interviewed.

This chapter has described, in detail, the various emic and etic methodologies used in the father-infant study. This is the first child

TABLE 10. Birth Questionnaire

The Birth
1. Where did you give birth? A) forest; B) village
2. What location? A) in hut; B) just behind hut; C) in forest; D) other (describe)
3. What season was it? A) honey; B) caterpillar; C) rainy; D) dry; E) other (describe)
4. How many people were there? A) many; B) one or two
5. Who was there? List names
6. Any younger children there?
7. Any males at birth—adults or children?
8. Who was first person to hold baby?
9. Who cut the cord?
10. What was the cord cut with?
11. How far up was it cut?
12. What was done with the baby after the birth? Describe.
13. Was the baby taken to the hut after birth? By whom?
14. How long before you arrived to hut where baby waited?
15. After birth when did lactation begin?
16. Has another woman ever nursed the baby?
17. What time of day did labor start and what time of day did you give birth?
18. Was the birth easy or difficult?

Protection
19. Was the baby given a "cord" (*mokodi*) the day of or day after birth?
20. When was baby given first cord? Who made it? Where was it placed?
21. Has the infant worn any other cords during its life?

Support
22. Did father stay home day after birth?
23. Who brought and made food for you?
24. Who collected firewood and water?
25. Where did husband and other children sleep after birth?
26. Did/does anyone else help if baby cries in the middle of the night?
27. How many days did you stay in the hut after birth?
28. After how many days did you go on a net hunt?

Taboo foods
29. At the end of the interview, the mother was asked if any of sixteen foods that were known to be taboo for at least some people were taboo for her. (If a person ate a taboo food, it caused the infant to get sick and possibly die.) After identifying her own taboo foods, the mother was asked if the same foods were taboo for the father. Later ten of the sixteen fathers were asked about their taboo food from the list of sixteen, and if they were the same as his wife. Aka and scientific name of taboo foods questioned:

TABLE 10—*Continued*

A. *senge*. Cephalophus leucogaster	H. *ngouya*. Potamochoerus porcus
B. *mbom*. Cephalophus dorsalis	I. *njoku*. Loxondonta cyclotis
C. *ekadi*. Manis tetradactyla	J. *esadu*. Cercocebus galeritus agilis
D. *assumba*. or *gbe*. Forest rat	K. *boka*. or other *tsui*. any fish
E. *gbeti*. Cercopithecus ascanius schmidti	L. *nau*. Colobus pennanti oustaleti
	M. *bimba*. Cephalophus silvicultor
F. *ngata*. Cercocebus albigena	N. *bongo*. Bocercus euryceros
G. *kalu*. Colobus guereza occidentalis	O. *njomba*. Trgelaphus spekei gratus

TABLE 11. Adolescent Questionnaire

1. Describe your parental history. Who raised you? Did you have stepfather/ mother?
2. Briefly, how was your relationship with the stepparent or second wife of your father?
3. Did you ever spend more than two moons with relatives other than your parents?
4. Is it necessary for you to give food to the family or camp or do you only collect/hunt for yourself?
5. Where do you sleep now?
6. If you have a choice, would you rather sleep with your mother or father, or does it make a difference?
7. Do you remember having to stop feeding from your mother's breast? Was it stopped by your mother or did you stop on your own?
8. Who was most kind to you while you were growing up?
   A) mother; B) father; C) both; D) other
9. Who played more with you when you were a *mona*?
   A) mother; B) father; C) both; D) other
10. Is your relationship with your: A) father; B) mother:
    A) better; B) worse than when you were a *mona*?
11. Who gets angry at you more often?
    A) mother; B) father; C) equal; D) other
12. Has your mother or father ever hit you? Why?
13. Whom do you have stronger sentiments for?
    A) mother; B) father; C) same; D) other
14. If you are hungry, whom do you tell?
    A) mother; B) father; C) other
15. If you are sick, who is more sympathetic?
    A) mother; B) father; C) other

(*continued*)

TABLE 11—*Continued*

16. Did you feel pain while getting your teeth pointed? If so, who was more sympathetic?
    A) mother; B) father; C) other
17. If you have a *mokandja* in your feet, whom do you prefer to cut them out?
    A) mother; B) father; C) other
18. Boys only—after circumcision, and if painful, who was more sympathetic?
    A) mother; B) father; C) other
19. Why do mothers, not fathers, primarily wash babies?
20. Sometimes men change positions on the net hunt, why?
21. Can you go to village/forest alone or with friends your age, or do you ask parents or other person?

TABLE 12. Parental Questionnaire

Experiences and feelings about own parents
1. Describe your parental history—who raised you, did you have a stepfather/mother, was your father ever polygynous?
2. Briefly, how was your relationship with your stepparent or second wife of your father?
3. What relative/family/friends do you now like to live near?
4. Did you ever spend more than two moons with relatives other than parents (e.g., grandparents)?
5. Do you remember having to stop breast feeding? Was it stopped by your mother or did you stop it on your own?
6. What stage of your childhood (*molope, djosi, mona, bokala/ngondo*) was the: A) most enjoyable; B) most difficult stage for you and your: A) mother; B) father?
7. Do you have stronger sentiments now for your? A) mother; B) father; C) equal; D) other
8. When you were sick as a child (*mona*), who was more sympathetic?
   A) mother; B) father; C) equal; D) other
9. When you were hungry as a *mona*, who generally got you some food?
   A) mother; B) father; C) other
10. When you had your teeth pointed, was it painful? If so, who was more sympathetic?
    A) mother; B) father; C) both; D) other
11. Were your parents ever mean to you? Describe. Ever hit you?
12. Who got angry at you more often when you were a *mona*? A) mother; B) father; C) other

TABLE 12—*Continued*

Experiences and feelings about own children

13. What does/did your child do that makes you very: A) happy; B) sad?
14. What time during your child's life has been your: A) favorite; B) most difficult?
15. Have you ever hit your children? For what?
16. What season of the year are you with your children: A) most; B) least?
17. What work/task do you enjoy doing: A) most; B) least with your *molope*?
18. If a: A) father; B) mother takes very: A) good; B) bad care of his/her *molope* what sorts of things would he/she do?
19. Who is more kind to children—women or men—and why?
20. If a *mona* is crying because he/she just fell down, who can better comfort the child? A) mother; B) father; C) equal; D) other person
21. If you ask: A) *mona*, B) *ngondo/bokala*, to get water and he/she refuses, what do you do?
22. Are there differences between a: A) boy; B) girl brought up without a father (given two situations): A) father dies; B) father leaves for another woman?
23. When a father goes to village or on a spear or crossbow hunt for many days or a moon, is it more difficult for wife and children to get food?
24. What things do village parents do with their children that you think are very: A) good; B) bad?

TABLE 13. Responsibility Questionnaire: "Who Has Primary Responsibility in the Given Situations?"

Everyone in family available

1. Who cleans *molepe* after urination?
2. Who cleans *molepe* after defecation?
3. Who finds healer if *molepe* has *elika ngombe*?
4. Who gives *dibinda* meat to eat?
5. Who sings to *molepe* if wakes up and cries in middle of night?
6. Who dances with *molepe* at *mabo* dance?
7. Who holds *molepe* while resting on net hunt?
8. Who carries *molepe* while family moves from village to forest camp?
9. Who washes *molepe* of five moons?
10. Who cleans lice from *dibinda* hair?
11. If a *mona* picks up *dibinda* and accidentally drops *dibinda* and *dibinda* cries, who goes to soothe *dibinda*?

Mother absent

12. If mother is very ill, who watches *dibinda*?
13. If mother is working in manioc field of villager, who watches *dibinda*?

(*continued*)

TABLE 13—*Continued*

14. Whom is mother most likely to give *molepe* to if she is busy cooking?
15. Whom is mother most likely to give *molepe* to if she has to go collect water?
16. Whom is mother likely to give *molepe* to on net hunt while she sits and cracks *piyu* nuts?
17. Who is most likely to carry/hold *molepe* on return from net hunt when mother is tired plus has a full basket of meat?

Mother and father absent
18. Who watches *dibinda* if both parents have left camp to collect *botende*?
19. If father is on spear hunt and mother leaves camp to collect water, who watches *dibinda*?
20. If mother and father are very tired after net hunt, whom will they give *dibinda* to to hold/watch?
21. If *dibinda* is hungry and mother and father are gone, who feeds *dibinda*?
22. If *dibinda* is playing in camp and parents are gone and a snake is seen in camp, who picks up *dibinda*?
23. If a mother leaves a *dibinda* inside the net on the ground to chase a *mosome* and *dibinda* cries, who takes care of *dibinda* (father also helping to get *mosome*)?
24. In early morning if father goes to look for honey and mother goes to collect firewood, who watches *dibinda*?
25. If *dibinda* is playing near hut and both parents are gone and an unfamiliar villager walks into camp and *dibinda* cries, who goes to get *dibinda*?

Note: molepe = infant, unable to crawl; *dibinda* = infant and able to crawl, but not able to walk; *mona* = child

development study to use father focal sampling techniques and to conduct observations in the evening. The next chapter begins to reveal the results of these methodologies and attempts to answer some of the following questions: how involved are Aka fathers in infant care, when are they most likely to provide infant care, and if they are not involved in infant care what are they doing?

TABLE 14. Aka Adults, Adolescents, and Children Questions as to How They Learned These Fifty Skills

1. net hunt—actively participate in net hunt
2. make string—make *kusa* for net
3. make net—make *boukiya* (for communal net hunt)
4. chase in net—chase *mboloko* (small duiker-Cephalophus monticola into net)
5. kill in net—kill *mosome* (large duiker-Cephalophus callipygus) once in net
6. wash net—wash net of malevolent spirits with *mousousie* (traditional medicine)
7. spear-hunt—hunt with spear on net hunt
8. make crossbow—make *mbano* alone
9. make poison—make *ndemele* (poison) for crossbow arrows
10. elephant hunt—hunt with spear on elephant hunt
11. identify monkey—identify sounds/behaviors of *kima esadu* (Cercocebus galeritus agilis)
12. find *koko*—identify *koko* (leaves of Gnetum sp.)
13. find honey—locate and retrieve honey from top of large tree
14. find fruit—find *botende* (species unknown)
15. find mushrooms—identify edible mushrooms
16. find nuts—find *piyu* nuts (Irvingia gabonesis)
17. carry basket—carry *yukwa* (collection basket)
18. digging stick—use digging stick to find *ignames*
19. climb tree—climb large tree with liana to get honey
20. find *igname*—identify and extract *ekuli* (Dioscorea lieorechtsiana) or other *igname*
21. vine water—collect water from forest liana
22. make *koko*—preparation of *koko* by shredding
23. prepare manioc—make manioc into flour
24. palm wine—prepare palm tree for *mbolu* drinking (type of procedure to get wine at base of tree)
25. ax tree—cut tree to get firewood
26. build fire—build fire without help
27. build cabin—build hut (for females) or hunting cabin (for males)
28. make ax—make ax handle
29. plant manioc—know method for preparing manioc branches for planting
30. bathe infant—bathe infant of three months or less
31. soothe infant—soothe infant that is crying and mother is gone
32. carry in sling—carry infant in sling on net hunt
33. carry on back—carry older child (*mona*, a 3–4 year old) on back
34. nonaggression—train child not to hit another child
35. *ekila* medicine—make traditional medicine for infant with *ekila* (convulsions)

(*continued*)

TABLE 14—*Continued*

36. *mokodi* amulet—make *mokodi* (cord woven from special vines) for good luck or protection
37. hold newborn—hold infant of five days
38. infant smile—make infant of four months smile
39. feed infant—feed food to infant of five months
40. in-laws—directions on appropriate behavior for living in camp of spouse (time of bride service for males and after brideservice for females)
41. sexual behavior—intercourse with mate
42. share *mboloko*—divide *mboloko* (small duiker) with others
43. share elephant—divide an *njoku* (elephant) with others
44. share honey—divide honey with others
45. *tuma* skills—powers and knowledge of *tuma* (great elephant hunter)
46. *nganga* skills—powers and knowledge of *nganga* (traditional healer)
47. dance *libanda*—type of dance for enjoyment
48. dance *djengi*—type of dance done after elephant kill (of great ritual significance)
49. hunt songs—sing while walking to net hunt
50. dance *elanda*—type of dance for enjoyment

CHAPTER 4

The Level and Context of Father Involvement

This chapter examines the levels of active and passive involvement of Aka fathers in various social and economic contexts. Four measures are examined: holding, proximity, availability, and nearest neighbor to father. Holding (called carrying in most other anthropological studies; Denham 1974; Hames 1988) is probably one of the better measures of the father's level of infant involvement because the father is actively engaged with the infant; he is expending energy on the infant instead of using it in other activities. Numerous studies have demonstrated that infant holding/carrying results in substantial energy (often measured in calories) costs for the caregiver (Lee 1979; Hurtado 1985; Peacock 1985). By contrast, passive involvement measures may not require direct energy investment but presume that the father is altering his behavior for the infant. Recent ethological studies have also indicated that holding is a significant factor for infant survival in populations, such as the Aka Pygmies, where infant mortality rates are high (LeVine 1977, 1989). Low infant mortality is a relatively recent phenomenon in industrialized populations, while infant mortality in highly industrialized nations ranges from 2–6 percent (Babchuk, Hames, and Thompson 1985). African Pygmy infant mortality rates range from 15 to 33 percent (Cavalli-Sforza 1986, chap. 2; Neuwelt-Truntzer 1981; Weiss 1973). Holding purportedly provides psychological comfort (Altman 1980) as well as protection from environmental factors such as predators, temperature changes, intraspecific aggression, and accidents (Bowlby 1969; Freedman 1974). It may also be a mechanism permitting the transmission of information from mothers to infants (Konner 1977). A limitation of these earlier studies is that generally only mother-infant contact has been considered. We know that compared to mothers, fathers in most nonindustrialized populations infrequently hold infants, assist in childcare, or even stay around infants (Whiting and Whiting 1975; and see table 42). Little is known about the social and environmental conditions under which fathers hold or carry the infants, or the differences and similarities between mothers' and fathers' caretaking styles (to be considered in the next chapter).

The last three measures of Aka father involvement (proximity, availability, and nearest neighbor to father) are all passive measures of father investment. They are "passive" measures in that the father may not be expending energy directly in the involvement, but the father's behavior may influence the infant's survival as well as its emotional and social development. An available father may enhance an infant's chances for survival if the infant is injured or threatened by a dangerous animal (snake, leopard, ants, or other insects). A nearby father also means that he is more likely to be transmitting cultural knowledge (either by direct instruction or by providing a model for the infant to observe and imitate). For a father to be within 1 m of an infant (proximity) suggests some preference by the father to be near the infant. Proximity and availability have been used as indicators of indirect paternal involvement in both human (Whiting and Whiting 1975; Borgerhoff Mulder and Milton 1985; Munroe and Munroe 1971) and nonhuman (e.g., Taub 1985) populations. Nearest neighbor to father (individual nearest to father, but within 10 m, and not held by the father) has never been used as a measure of paternal involvement. It has been employed as an observational measure to help determine the social sphere of a particular individual (Bailey 1985). In this study it provides further data on the physical distance between father and infant during the day.

HOLDING

Over the 264 hours of continuous focal observation, Aka fathers held their infants 8.7 percent of the time, or about one hour of father-holding during a twelve-hour (6 A.M. to 6 P.M.) observation period. Timed interval and spot observations were remarkably similar (8.5 percent for the former, and 8.3 percent for the latter). Figure 2 demonstrates that when one controls for age and general setting (forest versus village), one finds a gradual decrease in father-holding with age, which one would expect since infants are held less as they grow older. Figure 2 also indicates no significant differences in how often fathers held infants in the village and forest contexts.

Significant differences were found when specific settings within each of the two general contexts were examined. Figure 3 indicates that fathers were much more likely to be holding their infant in the camp than on the net hunt or in the village fields (see pls. 6–10). Figure 2 indicates there was no overall difference between father-holding in the village and forest, yet figure 3 suggests that fathers in the two forest contexts held their infants more than fathers in the two comparable village contexts. The inconsistency is a consequence of forest fathers spending a smaller percentage of their day in camp when father-holding is greatest. Fathers in the forest spent 29 percent of their day (6 A.M. to 6 P.M.) in the camp and 71 percent of their time on the hunt, while fathers in the village spent on average 52 percent of their time in the camp and 48 percent of their time outside the camp. Figure 2 does not take into account the total time fathers spent in each of the contexts.

Table 15 breaks down the two forest settings—in camp and on the net hunt—by age and compares father-holding to mother-holding and holding by others. Table 16 identifies the "others" who were holding the infant. Considering age and setting, fathers spent the most time holding one-to-four-month-old infants in the forest camp. On the net hunt, mothers were the main caretakers; fathers and others infrequently held the infant in this setting. The one to four month olds were held essentially all the time in both settings,

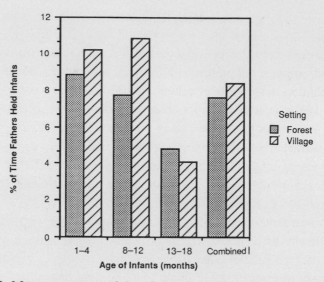

Fig. 2. Mean percentage of time fathers held their infants in two settings

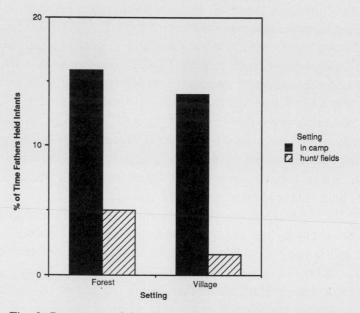

Fig. 3. Percentage of time fathers held infants in four contexts

while older infants were held about half the time in the camp and more than 90 percent of the time on the net hunt. This lends support to the notion that holding is performed to protect the infant from predators, snakes, and accidents. These dangers are more pronounced in remote forest locations on the hunt than in the camp clearing, and as a result infant holding is almost constant during this time.

Occasionally, it was difficult to tell if the parent was more inter-

TABLE 15. Mean Percentage of Time Mother, Father, and Others Held Focal Infant during Daylight Hours in Two Forest Contexts: In Camp and on the Net Hunt

Age of Infant (in months)	Mother	Father	Others	Total
	Forest Camp			
1–4	51.0	22.0	27.0	100.0
8–12	45.3	11.2	2.3	58.8
13–18	31.8	14.3	9.4	55.5
	Net Hunt			
1–4	87.3	6.5	6.2	100.0
8–12	87.8	5.9	0.0	93.7
13–18	88.9	2.4	1.1	92.4

TABLE 16. Holding by Others

Caregiver	% of Others' Time Held	Sex of Caregiver	% of Time Held in That Category
Grandparents	25.4	Female	99
		Male	1
Older brothers and sisters	12.8	Male	51
		Female	49
Brothers or sisters of mother or father	10.0	Male	37
		Female	63
In-laws or other adults	34.7	Male	42
		Female	58
Adolescent and young cousins	17.1	Female	99
		Male	1
Total	100.0		

ested in the protection of the infant or capturing game. Several instances were recorded where the mother holding the infant placed the infant alone on the ground and ran to capture the animal. The infant was left alone about 10 m from the parent, often crying, until the parent killed the animal. In instances where large (25–75 kg), potentially dangerous game were captured, it made sense to leave the infant at some distance, but usually the game weighed less than 6 kg. Instead of bringing the infant close to the net where the capture took place and where it would be possible to see the infant, the mothers said they preferred to be unencumbered so they could run faster and make sure the game did not get away.

Table 15 also demonstrates the relative consistency of father-holding. Regardless of the infant's age, about 20 percent of the time *the infant was held* in the camp and about 6 percent of the total time the infant was held on the net hunt the infant was held by its father (e.g., the eight-to-twelve-month-old infants were held 58.8 percent of the time in the forest camp, and the fathers held the infants about one-fifth of this time [11.2 percent of the time]).

Aka fathers do not assist in infant care while engaged in economic activity outside the village camp because male and female subsistence activities do not overlap; father cannot take care of the infant because he is not near the infant. (The infant goes with the mother because of the frequent nursing.) While residing in the forest, however, fathers do have opportunities to assist in infant holding since male and female subsistence activities overlap, but seldom do they help out. They were most likely to help out by transporting the infant back to camp after the net hunt. Aka frequently gave two explanations for the lack of father holding on the hunt: (*a*) Holding an infant made it more difficult to run after game, and (*b*) men were faster runners than women. One parent had to carry the infant on the net hunt while the other parent had to be free to chase game. Since men were faster runners, they should be free to run after game with the spear. Neither men nor women mentioned nursing the infant as a constraint. Aka women did not appear to be that slow; they were always faster than I. But, as mentioned earlier, women next to the net often put their infants down on the ground to run after game; a clear indication that infant holding constrained their running and, consequently, their hunting ability.

AVAILABILITY

Holding is an active form of father involvement while availability is one type of passive involvement, but is there a relationship between the two? If fathers are near their infants more frequently (i.e., available), do they hold their infants more often? Tables 17–19 summarize the father availability data. In comparing the general village versus forest contexts (table 17), fathers residing in the forest were much more available to their infants than were village fathers: While residing in the forest, fathers were within earshot 85 percent of the day, while a movement to the village meant a father would not be near his infant 54 percent of the day.

In comparing the availability and holding data, one finds that a father who is near his infant more often *does not* necessarily hold the infant more often. Fathers in the forest were available more often than fathers in the village yet held their infants just as frequently as fathers in the village. Figure 4 shows more specifically that fathers in the forest were near their infants (within view or hearing distance) 80 percent of the time on the net hunt, yet they infrequently held the infants in this setting. By comparison, fathers

TABLE 17.   Comparison of Father's Availability in Forest and Village Settings

Setting	Within Visual Range				Within Hearing Range (but not within visual range)				Out of Area			
	N	Mean	SD	SE	t-scores	N	Mean	SD	SE	t-scores	N	Mean	SD	SE	t-scores
Forest	15.0	63.6	15.2	4.1		15.0	21.9	7.2	1.9		15.0	14.5	10.4	2.8	
					3.3*					8.4*					6.9*
Village	6.0	42.9	10.3	4.7		6.0	3.4	2.8	1.3		6.0	53.7	11.0	5.0	

Notes: N = number of all-day observations. Mean scores are the average percentages of time fathers were available during daylight hours (6 A.M. to 6 P.M.). *$p < .005$ (19 df).

81

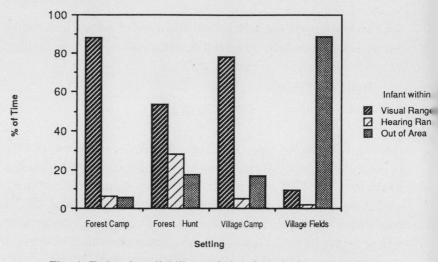

Fig. 4. Fathers' availability to their infants in four contexts

living in the village and working outside the camp were near their infants only 12 percent of the time. The significant differences in father availability in the forest versus the village setting were a consequence of different subsistence activities undertaken while residing in the forest or village. Net hunting enabled fathers to be as near their infants as the mothers, who usually transported the infant and assisted with the family net. In the village, Aka obtained vegetable foods by providing labor to the farming Ngandu. Ngandu male and female subsistence activities seldom overlap, as Aka males help Ngandu males and Aka females help Ngandu females. As a result of the divergent activities, fathers were less available to their infants. Also, while in the village, Aka males often left the camp at the first sign of dawn to search for palm wine (sap of the palm tree) that accumulated in special trees during the night. Small groups of men often did not return to camp until mid-morning, thus decreasing further their availability to their infants.

Table 18 compares fathers availability in the forest with the availability of mothers. Although Aka fathers are very available to their infants, mothers are essentially always available. Table 19 examines father availability as it relates to the age of the infant and indicates

TABLE 18. Comparison of Father and Mother Availability in Forest Setting

	Within Visual Range				Within Hearing Range				Out of Area			
Parent	N	Mean	SD	SE	t-scores	N	Mean	SD	SE	t-scores	N	Mean	SD	SE	t-scores
Father	6.0	92.7	8.0	3.6	5.3*	6.0	2.0	3.9	0.9	4.5*	6.0	5.2	7.4	3.3	2.2**
Mother	15.0	63.6	15.2	4.1		15.0	21.9	7.2	1.9		15.0	14.5	10.4	2.8	

Notes: N = number of all-day observations. Mean scores are the average percentages of time fathers or mothers were available during daylight hours (6 A.M. to 6 P.M.). *p < .005 (19 df); **p < .025 (19 df).

that father availability during infancy does not change significantly over time.

PROXIMITY

Tables 20–22 examine the frequency that Aka fathers were within 1 m of their infants during daylight hours. To make proximity a measure independent from holding, to be coded as within proximity the father could not be holding the infant. Also, unlike the holding and availability data which are based on minute by minute observations, the proximity data are derived from 912 timed interval observations (every fifteen minutes) during the all-day infant and father focal observations.

Table 20 indicates that overall Aka fathers were within proximity of their infants 7.5 percent of the day. This figure is substantial given the fact that fathers were within proximity of any person in only 37.7 percent of the observations. If one considers only those

TABLE 19. Father Availability and Age of Infant

Age of Infant (in months)	N	Mean	SD
1–4	6.0	65.1	25.4
8–12	5.0	71.0	21.3
13–18	4.0	71.1	20.6

Note: N = number of father-infant dyads.

observations where the father was within proximity of anyone, infants would be within proximity 20 percent of the time. But why are fathers within proximity, and in which setting? Seventy-two percent of the time the father was within proximity because the mother who was holding the infant was also within proximity. The

TABLE 20. Mean Percentage of Time Fathers Were Within Proximity of Focal Infants

Age of Infant (in months)	N	Mean	SD
1–4	6.0	5.8	6.6
8–12	5.0	7.7	6.1
13–18	4.0	10.1	7.9
Total	15.0	7.5	6.6

Notes: N = number of father-infant dyads. Mean = mean percentage of time during daylight hours father within proximity of infant.

TABLE 21. Mean Percentage of Time Fathers in Forest and Village Setting Were Within Proximity of Their Infants

Observational Setting	N	Mean	SD	SE	t
Forest	9.0	4.0	4.3	1.5	
					3.0*
Village	6.0	12.9	5.7	2.6	

Notes: N = number of father-infant dyads. Mean = mean percentage of time fathers were within proximity of their infant during daylight hours. * = $p < .01$ (14 df)

TABLE 22. Comparison of Father and Mother Proximity to Their Infant in Forest Setting

Infant Age (in months)	Mean Percentage of Time in Proximity to Infant	
	Mother	Father
1–4	4.1	1.6
8–12	20.7	4.1
13–18	18.3	8.5

remaining 28 percent of father-infant proximity observations were with the thirteen-to-eighteen-month-old infants. Father-infant proximity occurred almost exclusively in the camp setting (92 percent of observations), and 64 percent of all father-infant proximity observations were observed in the village context. These results are not surprising given Aka activity patterns and the setting of the observed proximity behavior. On the net hunt, a father is frequently available (see above) to his infant but seldom comes within 1 m of his wife who is holding the infant, while in camp a father often sits in front of the hut near his wife, who is holding the infant. The significant differences between proximity in the forest and village settings demonstrated in table 21 also reflect Aka activity patterns in these two settings. Since proximity occurs more in the camp setting, and village fathers are in the camp much more of the day than are forest fathers (52 percent of time for village fathers versus 29 percent of time for forest fathers), it is likely that village fathers would be within proximity of the infant more frequently.

Table 20 also suggests that there is an inverse relationship between holding and proximity. Young infants are held frequently but are less frequently in proximity, while older infants are held less but are within proximity more frequently. Table 22 compares mothers' and fathers' time in proximity to the infants in the forest setting, and as with holding and availability, mothers were in proximity to their infants much more frequently than were fathers.

NEAREST NEIGHBOR

Nearest neighbor data provide another measure of father involvement. This offers another measure of the "proximity maintenance" behavior of the father, which might allow him to help out in direct childcare or transmit important cultural knowledge. Like the proximity measure, the nearest neighbor data are based upon interval observations; unlike the proximity data, the nearest neighbor data are based only on father focal observations ($N = 610$ interval observations). Nearest neighbor is an independent measure from holding but not from the proximity measure. That is, if the father was holding his infant, the infant would not be coded as the father's nearest neighbor, but if the infant was within 1 m of the father, the infant would also be coded as the nearest neighbor.

Table 23 shows that the infant was the nearest neighbor to the father 18.6 percent of the time. The nearest neighbor data have three similarities to the proximity data: (1) the overall figure is more substantial than it first appears as fathers had a nearest neighbor (person within 10 m) in only 83 percent of all observations; (2) an infant was slightly more likely to be the father's nearest neighbor as the infant's age increased; and, (3) in 67 percent of the observations the infant was nearest neighbor because the mother (who was also coded as nearest neighbor) was holding the infant.

The nearest neighbor data are markedly different from the proximity data in three ways: (1) as demonstrated in table 24, there is no significant difference in the percentage of time the infant is the nearest neighbor to the father in the forest and village settings, and the pattern is just the opposite of that found with proximity (i.e., infant is nearest neighbor in forest setting, but within proximity more frequently in village setting); (2) the majority of infant as nearest neighbor observations came from the forest setting (66.9 percent) rather than the village setting; and, (3) a majority (65 percent) of the infant as nearest neighbor observations in the forest setting were observed during the net hunt rather than in the camp.

TABLE 23. Mean Percentage of Time Focal Infant Was Nearest Neighbor to Father

Age of Infant (in months)	*N*	Mean	SD
1–4	6.0	14.5	9.9
8–12	5.0	19.0	5.1
13–18	4.0	24.1	5.2
Total	15.0	18.6	8.0

Notes: *N* = number of father-infant dyads. Mean = mean percentage of time focal infant was nearest neighbor to father during daylight hours.

86

TABLE 24. Mean Percentage of Time Focal Infant Was Nearest Neighbor to Father in Forest and Village Settings

Observational Setting	N	Mean	SD	SE	t
Forest	9.0	21.0	8.2	2.9	
					1.4
Village	6.0	15.0	6.7	3.0	

Notes: N = number of father-infant dyads. Mean = mean percentage of time focal infant was nearest neighbor to father.

Overall, comparing proximity and nearest neighbor data indicates father-infant proximity is most likely to occur in the village camp, while the infant as nearest neighbor to father is most likely to occur in the forest on the net hunt.

GENERAL ACTIVITY OF FATHERS

One goal of the study was to try and determine what other activities fathers were engaged in if they were not performing childcare tasks. Were fathers who did less childcare spending more time hunting or in the manufacture of better equipment for hunting? Were fathers who did substantially more caretaking than other fathers on leisure days doing little else? Were the fathers who did less infant caretaking spending more time in status promotion or maintenance?

Table 25 gives an overview of father activity in forest and village settings. These data are based upon interval coding ($N = 988$) of fathers during all-day observations. The data are interesting in a number of respects. Fathers did about the same amount of childcare and manufacturing (e.g., making string for nets) in both contexts. With regard to overall productive labor, forest fathers did considerably more. Forest fathers spent 51 percent of their time in pursuit of game, while village fathers only spent 17.8 percent of their time gardening or doing other labor for a villager. If village labor time is divided between active and rest time, and rest time is subtracted from the overall time Aka fathers are in the village fields working for villagers, Aka fathers actively "work" only 10.5 percent of the day. Aka fathers in the village spent most of their time visiting, searching for palm wine, and just sitting idly around camp. Forest fathers spent most of their days on the net hunt. About 25 percent of the time on the net hunt was spent resting.

Table 26 explores the questions raised above. The activities of fathers that frequently held their infants are compared with fathers who held their infants significantly less. Although the number of father-infant dyads used for comparison is admittedly few, the results do suggest some answers to the questions. First, fathers that did less childcare did not spend more time in hunting, garden labor, or in the manufacture of subsistence tools. In fact, less active fathers in the village actually did 50 percent less garden labor than the active caretaking fathers. This also indicates that fathers who were frequently holding their infants were not on "days off" or leisure days; they were actively engaged in subsistence activity. Second, there is some indication that less active fathers compensated the childcare time with visiting time. In both the village and forest settings less active fathers spent substantially more time talking and

TABLE 25. Mean Percentage of Time Fathers in Village and Forest Settings Engaged in Various Activities (Daylight Hours Only) ($N = 988$)

Activity	Forest[a]	Village[b]
Net hunt—active	51.0	0.0
Net hunt—rest	16.2	0.0
Manufacture	6.4	5.3
Search for palm wine	0.0	22.6
Garden or other labor for villager	0.0	17.8
Visiting with others	8.2	20.5
Infant care	8.8	8.2
Dancing	0.0	3.4
Eating	0.9	3.4
Hygiene	0.1	1.0
Idle	8.1	16.7

[a]Mean percentage of time father residing in forest engaged in this activity
[b]Mean percentage of time father residing in village engaged in this activity

visiting with other members of the camp. It will be demonstrated later that fathers usually talk to other males in the camp (see chap. 5). These few data may suggest that less active fathers are either engaged in more status promotion or maintenance or that they have a reason for spending more time visiting (e.g., they have more relatives to visit in the camp). These explanations will be explored further when intracultural variation is examined in chapter 7.

Fathers' Evening Activities

Most systematic observations were conducted during daylight hours, but some were made to obtain data on fathers' activities in camp after sundown. Table 27 summarizes the results of sixty-one spot observations in the forest context and twenty-five spot observations conducted in the village context between 6:30 P.M. and 9:00 P.M. The most striking result in regard to this study is the extensive amount of time fathers in both settings spent in childcare. Fathers on average spent about one-fifth of their evening in infant care

TABLE 26. How Fathers Who Held Their Infants Frequently Spent Their Time in Comparison Other Fathers

Amount of Infant Holdings[a]	N[b]	Village Activity				
		Manufacture	Palm Wine	Idle	Visit Others	Garden Labor
High	2.0	5.1	18.3	18.3	16.3	26.5
Average	4.0	5.6	24.8	15.9	22.6	13.5
		Forest Activity				
		Net hunt—active	Net hunt—rest	Manufacture	Visit Others	Idle
High	2.0	48.7	16.3	7.4	5.1	7.3
Average	7.0	51.6	16.1	6.1	9.0	8.4

[a]Fathers that held their infants nearly or greater than 15 percent of time during daylight hours (6 A.M. to 6 P.M.) are considered "high"; all other fathers held their infants less than 7 percent of time and are considered "average."
[b]Number of father-infant dyads

(usually holding a sleeping infant). Fathers in both settings spent about the same time eating, sleeping, manufacturing, and talking with others. As during daylight activity, village fathers had considerably more idle time than forest fathers. Forest fathers did almost twice as much dancing as village fathers.

No attempt was made to make systematic observations past 9:00 P.M. Aka were generally asleep, unless there was a dance, and I simply did not set time aside to stay up all night and record activity. Important activities do, of course, occur and future studies should examine activities during this time.

Casual observations were made during the night. Aka were most likely to sleep together in the same bed. Since Aka couples sleep together, proximity and holding measures should occur in 100 percent of the observations; that is, between 9:00 P.M. and 6:00 A.M., fathers would be either holding or within proximity of their infants. Infants often woke up during the night, and it was not unusual to hear a father humming and singing to the infant if it was fussing. If the infant was especially fussy, a father was more likely than a mother to take the infant outside of the hut and walk or dance with the infant.

This chapter has quantitatively described the level and context of Aka paternal infant care. Aka fathers are very intimate with their infants, especially in specific social and environmental contexts.

TABLE 27. Evening (6:30–9:00 P.M.) Activities of Fathers in Forest and Village Settings

Activity	Forest[a]	Village[b]
Manufacture	6.7	4.0
Talking with others	21.7	28.0
Infant care	23.3	16.0
Singing/dancing	15.0	8.0
Eating	10.0	8.0
Lying down/sleeping	20.0	20.0
Idle	3.3	16.0

[a]Mean percentage of time fathers residing in forest engaged in this activity
[b]Mean percentage of time fathers residing in village engaged in this activity

The next chapter considers the nature of father-infant interaction. How do fathers interact with their infants? How does their caretaking style differ from that of mothers and other caregivers?

CHAPTER 5

The Nature of Father Caregiving

How do Aka fathers interact with their infants? Is the father's style of caregiving different than the mother's? Do Aka fathers prefer to hold sons over daughters? Do infants fuss when they are being held by fathers? This chapter examines these and other questions that deal with the nature or quality of father-infant interaction.

The Aka father data do not support the contention discussed in chapter 1 that fathers are vigorous, rough-and-tumble playmates. Only one episode of physical play by a father was recorded during all 264 hours of systematic observation. In examining all infant focal observations (92 hours of observation) where mothers', fathers', and others' play could be directly compared, it was found that fathers never engaged in vigorous play, mothers played vigorously three times, and others played roughly with the infants nine times. Although the data are obviously meager, data regarding other caretakers are striking given the relative infrequency with which they held infants. Who are the "others" engaging in physical play with infants? Eight of the nine cases were performed by older (three-to-twelve-year-old) brothers and sisters of the infants. This is especially significant as brothers and sisters account for only 13 percent of the total time "others" held the infant (table 16).

Figure 5 examines the frequency of various activities mothers, fathers, and others engaged in while holding the infant. Fathers' activity data are based upon all-day father and infant focal observa-

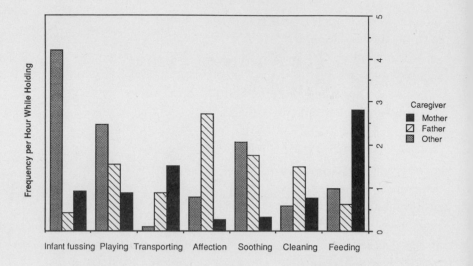

Fig. 5. Activities of caregiver while holding infant

tions (about 235 hours of observation), while mothers' and others' data are based upon all-day infant focal observations only (about 72 hours of observation). The data measure the frequency with which certain activities occurred while the parent held the infant; each episode was marked only once whether it lasted a few seconds or minutes. With these limitations in mind, the data do indicate different qualities of mothers, fathers and others holding (see pls. 11–12). Mothers were most likely to provide nourishment and transport the infant, while fathers were more likely to hug, kiss, or clean the infant as they were holding. Others were most likely to soothe a fussy infant or play with the infant while holding. Others provided more episodes of activity per hour than fathers and mothers combined. Fathers provided more episodes of activity than mothers per hour, but their episodes were briefer and more intense. Fathers held their infants 11.1 minutes per hold by comparison to mothers' 23.3 minutes per hold. Mothers were more inclined to invest in longer, more energetically demanding activities, such as transporting and nursing. Others were much more likely to have an

94

infant fuss while they were holding, and fathers were least likely to have an infant fuss while holding. The great amount of soothing provided by others was generally in response to the infant's fussing. Fathers' soothing was not in response to infant fussing and generally consisted of humming or singing softly. These data also suggest that it is others, not fathers, who are most likely to engage in play with the infant.

Tables 28 and 29 list the activities the father and mother engaged in while the father held his infant. The data are derived from 102 father holds that took place during the all-day father and infant focal observations. Following each father hold, the father's and the mother's primary activity during the hold was noted. Again, these are frequency rather than durational measures. The father and mother were usually idle during part of every hold, yet it was coded as such only if it was the primary activity.

Aka fathers provided "quality time" to their infants since in over one fourth of the holds the father did not engage in other activities and devoted his attention almost entirely to the infant. During most holds, the father participated in other activities. Although women are often characterized as being talkative, fathers in over one third of the episodes engaged in conversation with others, especially adult males, while holding the infant. With the exception of transporting the infant back from the net hunt, fathers were much less likely to hold the infant while engaged in economic activity than in social activity. This reinforces the earlier finding that fathers primarily held their infants while in camp—not in the forest or the fields, where they are usually engaged in economic activity. The father often held the infant while the mother was busy collecting firewood, preparing a meal, or net hunting (see table 29). This reflects the Aka conception of a good father—one who assists with infant care when the mother's workload becomes excessive.

Another method of delineating fathers' and mothers' caretaking styles has been used by Lamb (1977a) and was attempted in this study. Lamb found that American mothers and fathers picked up their infants for different reasons—mothers were more likely to pick

TABLE 28. Father's Activity While Holding Infant

Father's Activity	Relative Frequency Engaged in This Activity While Holding
Primary caretaking—no other activity and devotes near full attention to infant	0.26
Talking with other adult males	0.25
Talking with others besides adult males	0.12
Economic activity (making string, net hunting)	0.06
Transporting infant from net hunt	0.05
Idle	0.15
Eating or drinking	0.08
Other (preparing meals)	0.03

TABLE 29. What Mother Is Doing While Father Holds Infant

Mother's Activity	Relative Frequency Engaged in This Activity
Left camp to collect firewood or water	0.24
Food Preparation	0.32
House Maintenance (making and repairing)	0.07
Net Hunting	0.18
Idle	0.12
Other (talking to other, eating)	0.08

up the infants for caregiving purposes and fathers for playing. In this study, each time an Aka parent voluntarily picked up the infant, a purpose for this action was coded (caregiving, control, play, affection, infant request, caregiver desire, soothe, other). In a short time it became obvious that the results would be limited for the Aka seldom picked up the infant voluntarily: the infant was usually transferred from someone else or it initiated and completed the action itself by climbing onto the parent's lap. Only 176 instances of clearly parent-initiated holding were recorded. Figure 6 compares four reasons why parents and others picked up their infants. (Only those purposes in which there were at least twenty-five cases are shown; for instance, in only three cases was an infant picked up to play with, so that reason was not included in fig. 6). There were a number of significant differences. Most frequently, mothers picked up the infant for caregiving (mother-father $\chi^2 = 8.02, p < .005[1$ df]); fathers picked up the infant because the infant made some

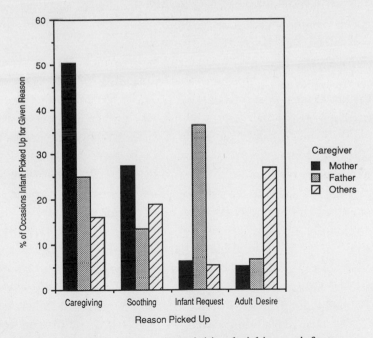

Fig. 6. Reasons why caregivers initiated picking up infants

gesture or summons to be picked up (mother-father $\chi^2 = 20.38$, $p < .005$ [1 df]); while others picked up the infant simply because they wanted to (other-father $\chi^2 = 6.10$, $p < 0.025$[1 df]). The data indicate that infants frequently seek out fathers and that fathers do not pick up infants to play with them.

In the American studies, "play" has been an important behavior for differentiating mothers' and fathers' caretaking styles. Researchers have demonstrated that fathers may not play with the infant any more than mothers do, but fathers' style of play is characteristically more physical, rough-and-tumble, and unpredictable, while mothers' play is more conventional (pat-a-cake, peek-a-boo) and toy-mediated. All instances of Aka infant-caretaker play were coded into one of four categories of play: major physical (rough-and-tumble, total body movement, chase); minor physical (tickling, nibbling, slight bouncing in lap); object-mediated (three subtypes: parallel, stimulus, and tease); and face-to-face. Each episode of face-to-face play with infants one to four months of age was further coded with one to three descriptive codes from a list of six (proximal, distal, verbal, physical, visual, tactile).

Most Aka infant play occurred in early infancy and was primarily of the face-to-face type. Of the 238 instances of play observed in the infant focal observations (102 hours of observation), 72 percent occurred in the one-to-four-month age group, 15 percent in the eight-to-twelve-month age group, and 13 percent in the thirteen-to-eighteen-month age group. Sixty-five percent of the one to four month olds' play was of the face-to-face type. Since the number of play episodes among the older infants was so few, only one-to-four-month-old infants' play episodes will be examined in detail.

Figure 7 summarizes mothers', fathers', and others' types of play with one-to-four-month-old infants. First, as demonstrated above, others engaged in *all* types of play more frequently than both mothers and fathers. Second, physical rough-and-tumble play was rare. The only significant difference between mother and father was in face-to-face play: fathers engaged in this type of play more frequently than mothers ($\chi^2 = 11.67$, $p < 0.005$[1 df]). Significance

98

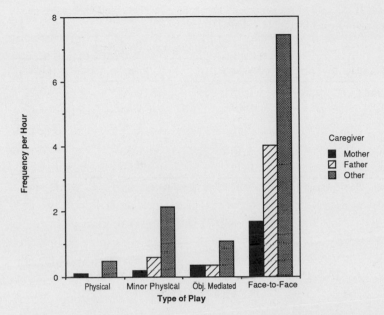

Fig. 7. Types of play while holding one-to-four-month-old infants

tests based on data from tables 30 and 31 indicated there were no significant differences between the types of face-to-face play that male and female infants received or between the types that mothers, fathers, and others provided.

TABLE 30. Types of Face-to-Face Play One-to-Four-Month-Old Infants Receive From Caretakers Holding or Within Proximity of the Infant

Type of Play	Relative Frequency	
	Male Infants	Female Infants
Proximal	0.24	0.20
Distal	0.09	0.15
Verbal	0.19	0.22
Physical	0.13	0.11
Visual	0.09	0.16
Tactile	0.25	0.16

Note: No significant differences were found ($p < .05$).

TABLE 31. Types of Face-to-Face Play Mothers, Fathers, and Others Provide Their One-to-Four-Month-Old Infants

	Relative Frequency		
Type of Play	Mothers	Fathers	Others
Proximal	0.25	0.20	0.21
Distal	0.09	0.14	0.13
Verbal	0.21	0.20	0.21
Physical	0.10	0.14	0.13
Visual	0.10	0.18	0.11
Tactile	0.24	0.16	0.21

Note: No significant differences were found ($p < .05$).

INFANT'S ATTACHMENT BEHAVIOR
TOWARD FATHER

Attachment, for its original theorist, John Bowlby (1969), was an affective bond that arose out of the infant's innate need for stable and consistent social response from a significant other. Drawing on observations of mother-infant bonding in nonhuman primates, Bowlby proposed that attachment to a caretaker evolved because it promotes the survival of the the altricial infant by protecting it from predators or exposure to the elements. Through behaviors that seek and attempt to maintain proximity, the infant elicits and signals a partnership with this significant other. Lack of an attachment figure (generally mother) or disruption of the attachment process results in "a blockage in the capacity to make deep relationships." (Bowlby 1969:xiii).

Behaviors that maintain or seek proximity can be interpreted as attachment behaviors. Among humans, attachment behaviors (generally to mother) emerge around six to nine months of age. The proximity attachment is demonstrated by the infant's protest when separated from a particular adult, as opposed to all adults. This separation is an innate "cue to danger" that elicits signaling behavior intended to restore proximity. These attachment behaviors have been described as approaching, reaching, touching, seeking to be held, and fussing for someone (Ainsworth 1977; Lamb 1981).

To understand the nature of the Aka father-infant relationship, it seemed important to measure attachment behaviors to fathers, especially as these compared to behaviors toward mothers. Previous studies of attachment in non-Western settings have utilized the structured "strange situation" to measure infant attachment (Ainsworth 1977; Konner 1977; Leiderman and Leiderman 1977). Basically, this method involves placing the infant in a room with toys and the individual(s) one is interested in measuring attachment to, and asking the individual(s) to leave the room to see if the infant demonstrates any attachment behaviors for the individual(s). Given my limited background with this technique, and my sense that it was not culturally appropriate (Aka infants are rarely left alone) and could cause unnecessary stress on infant and parents, I decided to measure attachment behaviors as they naturally occurred.

Table 32 summarizes the attachment behaviors ($N = 213$) demonstrated toward mothers, fathers, and others during all-day infant focal observations (the only observations where infant behaviors toward mother, father, and others could be directly compared). Since the aim was to compare attachment behaviors toward mothers and fathers, only those attachment behaviors that occurred while both the mother and father were within view of the infant were tabulated in table 32. When the mother or father was not present, the person tending the infant received most attachment behaviors. Eighty-five percent of all attachment behaviors occurred when both parents were within view of the infant. Infants clearly demonstrated most attachment behaviors toward mothers (54 percent of all attachment behaviors), but infants also often sought the attention of their fathers (24.3 percent). Infants, in fact, sought the proximity of their fathers more often than all "other" individuals combined (21.7 percent). The predominance of attachment behaviors toward mothers is not unexpected given the greater frequency mothers held (table 15), were available to (table 18) and within proximity of (table 22) their infants. Since mothers were on average three times more involved than fathers in holding and proximity, the number of attachment behaviors expressed toward mothers may in fact be considered comparatively low. But the pervasiveness of the mother is suggested by table 32. When infants fussed, for instance, it was almost exclusively for mother (85.2 percent). Infants were more likely to walk within 1 m of father or crawl into his lap. Infants did not fuss for mother simply so they could nurse: Only 18.5 percent of infant fussing toward the mother resulted in the mother nursing the infant, while 44.4 percent of infant fussing for mother resulted in the mother simply holding the infant.

Table 33 examines the effect of age on infants' attachment behaviors. The older infants (those able to walk) demonstrated more attachment behaviors overall (since their mobility increased substantially) and exhibited attachment behaviors to their fathers almost twice as frequently as the younger infants. The percentage of attachment behaviors toward mothers and others did not change significantly with age. Infants appear more interested in being near their fathers as they begin to walk and explore the environment for themselves.

TABLE 32.   Attachment Behaviors Expressed by Aka Infants to Mothers, Fathers, and Others

	Percentage of Attachment Behavior to		
Attachment Behavior	Mother	Father	Others
Touch (already in proximity)	58.3	13.9	27.8
Approach and touch	65.7	8.6	25.0
Crawls in lap (already in proximity)	75.0	25.0	0.0
Approach and crawls in lap	57.1	33.3	9.5
Seeks to be held	60.0	40.0	0.0
Approach	20.0	42.5	37.5
Fuss for	85.2	11.1	3.7
Proffer	56.2	31.2	12.5
Reaches for	0.0	25.0	75.0

TABLE 33.   Age Effects on Attachment Behaviors Expressed to Mothers, Fathers, and Others

Infants' Age (in months)	Percentage of Attachment Behaviors Expressed to			
	N^a	Mother	Father	Others
8–12	90	58.8	15.5	22.2
13–18	123	50.4	29.3	20.3

[a]Number of attachment behaviors observed

DESCRIPTIVE EXAMPLES

The above discussion of father-infant style of interaction is overwhelmingly quantitative. While essential to anthropological research, this approach sometimes makes it difficult to grasp the flow and context of social interaction. The following brief qualitative descriptions of infants' interactions with fathers were selected to represent, as best as possible, the quantitative results and to provide some examples of the sorts of childcare tasks fathers engage in.

Yopo and son Manda. At 7:05 A.M. Yopo's wife Bongbongo gets off the bed, where she was sitting holding Manda, their eight-month-old son, and starts to exit from the hut. While exiting she turns and hands Manda to Yopo, who is also sitting on the bed, and goes outside and begins replacing old leaves on the hut with new ones. As Yopo takes Manda into his lap he softly hums to the boy. Yopo gives Manda a piece of manioc he is eating. Bongbongo leaves camp to get water. Yopo continues to hum rhythmically to Manda as Manda reaches for and plays with a twig on the bed. Yopo lies down and puts Manda on his chest as he continues to hum. Manda sits on Yopo's chest and smiles and vocalizes to Yopo; Yopo returns the same. Yopo sits up on the bed as he places Manda on the ground. Manda stands up as he holds onto his father. Yopo lies down again and puts Manda back on his chest. First Yopo sings like they were on a net hunt, then he stands Manda on his chest. Manda sits down on Yopo's chest and cuddles up to Yopo's neck at which time Yopo puts a leaf on Manda's head and Manda squeals with joy. Yopo continued to sing softly and play with Manda for forty-two minutes. Bongbongo came back during this time; Yopo held Manda about twenty minutes after she had returned.

Kakao and daughter Bambiti. Two-month-old Bambiti is sitting in Kakao's lap outside their hut. Tengbe, Kakao's wife, is sitting idly about two meters away. Kakao has been holding Bambiti for about twelve minutes already. Kakao pours some water in his hand from a gourd, tilts Bambiti's head back, and gives her a drink. Kakao vocalizes and Bambiti returns the vocalization. Kakao stands Bambiti on his knee and lightly blows and kisses her neck. Bambiti smiles. Kakao puts Bambiti back in his lap, and Bambiti grabs his ear. At 8:55 A.M. it is about time to leave for the net hunt so Kakao puts on the infant sling, puts Bambiti in it, takes his spear out of the ground, puts on his small *sawala* (purse), and starts walking into the forest. Tengbe follows about fifteen meters behind carrying her basket. About three minutes into the forest Kakao stops, gives his spear to Tengbe, cleans some mucus from Bambiti's nose, and starts walking again carrying Bambiti and his *sawala*. Kakao sings and vocalizes to Bambiti as he walks. Tengbe and Kakao begin to sing together. Fifteen minutes into the forest Bambiti falls asleep as Kakao carries her. At 9:40 A.M., Kakao stops where some others have found a tree which they think may contain honey. Kakao gives Bambiti to Tengbe, who promptly starts nursing Bambiti. Kakao eventually helps cut down the tree, but no honey is found.

Ngaka and son Konvocation. Fifteen-month-old Konvocation is standing in the forest just behind the family hut playing alone on some tree branches. As he is playing, he decides to defecate but only a few meters from the hut. Konvocation walks over in front of the family hut and his mother and father see that he has defecated. Ndomu, his mother, is nursing the infant of Ndanga,

Konvocation's nineteen-year-old sister. Ngaka calls Konvocation over and he cleans the feces off of Konvocation with some leaves. Ngaka then finds the feces behind the hut and also cleans them up with some leaves. Ngaka sits back down in front of the hut and continues to make *kusa* (string for net). Konvocation walks towards Ngaka, puts his hand on Ngaka's leg, and watches Ngaka make *kusa*.

Mangata and daughter Samoli. It is 3:34 P.M. and Mangata has just returned to camp from searching the fields for palm wine. Mangata takes Samoli, his three-month-old daughter, from his half sister, Ndingu, and sits down with her in front of the family hut. Mangata looks at her genitals to see if they are clean and then wipes saliva from Samoli's mouth. He kisses Samoli on the cheek, and Samoli proceeds to urinate on him. Mangata waits for her to finish, then grabs a nearby cloth, and casually wipes the urine off his leg as he sings softly to Samoli. Mangata places Samoli in his lap again and talks with Nbangba and Botubu, two adult males in camp. He talks with them for ten minutes, when the infant begins to fuss. Mangata walks over to Gabaliki, his wife, who is making palm oil, and gives Samoli to her. Gabaliki nurses Samoli.

These brief descriptive examples demonstrate the intimacy of the father-infant relationship, the variety of infant caretaking tasks fathers perform, and some of the contexts in which father-holding and caretaking are likely to take place.

This chapter has rejected Western psychological characterizations of the father-infant relationship. Aka fathers are not vigorous with their infants and are better characterized by their affectionate and nurturing interaction with the infant. The chapter has also demonstrated that infants are clearly attached to their fathers. Older Aka infants sought out fathers more than any other adult besides the mother. In the previous two chapters the Aka have spoken through their actions. In anthropology, this is called the "etic" or outsider's perspective. In the next chapter Aka speak for themselves about fathers and fathers' roles. Anthropologists call this the "emic" or insider's perspective. How do Aka adults and children view their fathers? Do they perceive mothers and fathers differently?

CHAPTER 6

Aka Perceptions of Fatherhood

While the description of the father-infant relationship in the previous two chapters was based upon observational data, this chapter examines the relationship using interview data. Interview data provide a means of checking the observational data as well as a mechanism for exploring Aka parenting ideology. While human behavior is often adaptive from an evolutionary (i.e., reproductive strategies) or ecological (i.e., adaptation to an environment) viewpoint, an understanding of ideology is essential because it directs human actions. The previous chapters have described Aka actions; this chapter provides an understanding of the motivations for those actions from an Aka vantage point.

QUALITIES OF GOOD AND BAD PARENTS

Twenty Aka adults were interviewed separately about the qualities of good and bad mothers and fathers. Table 34 summarizes their responses. The qualities of a good mother or father were remarkably similar. Consistently providing food for the child, staying near and protecting the child, and loving the child were highly desirable qualities of both mothers and fathers. Providing child caretaking assistance to the mother while she was busy was seen as an additional important quality for fathers.

In contrast to the descriptions of "good" parents, the qualities of "bad" mothers and fathers were markedly different. Male and female adults overwhelmingly indicated that a "bad" father leaves his wife and infant frequently, stays away from the family for long periods, walks around looking for other women or another wife, or completely abandons the family. Such behavior was seldom mentioned for mothers and had a different meaning for them. A mother that abandoned an infant stayed in camp but left the infant alone; a father that abandoned an infant left the camp for long periods. Another striking contrast was the concern about hitting (actually slapping) children. Hitting children is looked down upon by Aka, and mothers are reported as more likely than others to engage in this behavior (see section on discipline later in this chapter). Consequently, "bad" mothers are often identified with this quality. There is also some indication that the mother has a greater responsibility for providing food. While this is an important quality of good mothers and fathers, failure to provide food is an especially distinguishing quality of bad mothers but is infrequently mentioned of bad

TABLE 34. Qualities Listed by Forty Aka Adults of Good and Bad Mothers and Fathers

Good Father	%	Good Mother	%
Provides regular food	30.3	Stays near and guards	28.5
Loves children	23.2	Provides regular food	26.5
Assists mother	17.8	Loves infant	16.3
Stays near and guards	16.1	Washes infant	6.2
Other qualities	12.5	Takes good care when sick	6.2
		Other qualities	16.3

Bad Father	%	Bad Mother	%
Abandons infant	40.0	Hits children	31.4
Hits children	15.5	Does not provide enough food	28.7
Does not share food	11.1	Leaves infant alone/abandons	11.4
Does not provide enough food	11.1	Does not wash infant	11.4
Does not help mother with childcare	8.9	Other qualities	17.1
Does not love infant	6.7		
Other qualities	6.7		

Note: % = percentage of adults that mentioned this quality.

fathers. An undesirable father was one who had food (honey was often mentioned here) but did not share it (he would eat it in the forest before returning to camp).

SENTIMENTS FOR PARENTS

Ngandu farmers, especially males, often told me of their warm sentiments for their mothers and their distant feelings for their fathers. Ngandu would go on and on about how they had a special closeness in their heart for their mothers. I wondered if Aka had any such sentiments and decided to systematically ask adolescents and adults if they had especially strong sentiments for their mother, father, or some other person. The responses were quite different from those of Ngandu villagers and the adolescent pattern was markedly different from the adults. Female adolescents felt the greatest sentiments for a female relative; only one of eight mentioned her mother, while three mentioned an older sister. Five of ten female adults, on the other hand, said they had strong sentiments for an older brother(s) (one other mentioned a paternal uncle, while three mentioned mother and father). Only one male adolescent of eight mentioned his father, none mentioned their mothers, and four mentioned their father and mother. Only two of ten male adults said they had greatest sentiments for their fathers, and none mentioned their mothers. Only one of the male adults said he had greatest sentiments for a female relative (the second wife of his father).

Two conclusions may be inferred. First, unlike the Ngandu, Aka do not have stronger feelings for mothers. Second, the differences between adolescents and adults reflect differences in support persons associated with stages in the domestic cycle. Older sisters and other females are important support and identity figures for adolescent females. Because mothers often ask their adolescent daughters to help with various tasks, the daughters travel to other camps and often prefer to live near older sisters who place few demands on them. Visiting also allows adolescent daughters to meet potential spouses. In contrast, older brothers or other male relatives provide critical support to adult women; even though a woman lives in the camp of her husband, her brothers visit and support her if she separates from her husband or has marital difficulties. For adult males, paternal relatives are especially important for economic support, and their feelings of sentiment reflect this interest.

SENTIMENTS FOR CHILDREN

Ten fathers and ten mothers were asked about: (1) behaviors they liked or disliked in their two-to-five-year-old children; (2) the stages of child development (their emic categories) and, (3) the infant caregiving tasks they enjoyed most and least. These are rather open-ended questions, but the results were interesting. Mothers and fathers had very similar responses about the behaviors in their children they liked and disliked. Six mothers and five fathers stated that they liked to see their children get along with others and strongly disliked seeing their children hit, argue, or fight with other children. Three fathers and two mothers did not like to see their children take food from others or eat all the food in the house. Three mothers and two fathers did not like it when their children cried or were sick. Two mothers reported enjoying watching their children laugh and smile, and two fathers liked it when their children listened to their requests.

Mothers and fathers differed substantially in their feelings about the different stages of child development and the infant caregiving tasks they enjoyed most and least. Eight fathers said they enjoyed all stages of child development while only four of ten mothers said they liked all stages equally well. One father said he did not like the *djosi* (mother pregnant with next child) stage because the child is always crying for food, and one father did not like infancy because it was necessary to always transport and clean the infant. Three mothers disliked infancy the most because the infant cried a lot, was sick more frequently, and had to be transported by the mother. Two mothers did not like adolescence because the children never listened to you. Two women mentioned that they especially liked early childhood.

Mothers and fathers currently with children under two were asked which infant caregiving tasks they enjoyed most and least. Five of eight men said no task was difficult or unpleasant while only two of eight women gave this opinion. Two fathers did not like to wash babies and one said it was difficult to get enough food for both mother and baby. Two mothers did not like transporting, two did not like it when the infant was sick and cried hard, one did not like breastfeeding, and one did not like the food taboos associated with infancy.

In terms of caregiving tasks that parents enjoyed, most men (five of eight) enjoyed dancing and singing to the infant while most mothers (five of eight) enjoyed washing the infant. Two mothers said they especially enjoyed nursing and three fathers said they especially enjoyed giving things to their infants (honey, woven bracelets).

Although the numbers are small, some patterns emerge. First, only one father singled out infancy as a period he did not enjoy. This is not surprising given the active involvement of fathers in infant care, but it is in striking contrast to numerous other cultures (including our own) in which fathers say they are not interested in children until they can speak with them or do things with them. Fathers in many cultures do not like infancy because they might have to clean up after the infant defecates (change a dirty diaper). The eight fathers that indicated there was no unpleasant task were specifically asked about cleaning up after the infant urinated or defecated on them (Aka do not use any form of diapers). All said it was no problem whatsoever. Second, the interview data demonstrated the concern about training for nonviolence, nonaggression and sharing.

FATHER AS DISCIPLINARIAN AND NURTURER

According to Lamb et al. 1983 and others (Clarke-Stewart 1980; Yogman 1982), the father's vigorous play develops attachment to the father and is the initial means of establishing social competence. Aka data tend to run counter to this hypothesis. The interview data

111

support the observational finding that the father's role cannot be characterized by its physical playfulness. Only three of sixteen adolescents said their fathers were most playful with them when they were a child; four mentioned their mothers as more playful; and two said both mother and father were playful. Fathers seldom engaged in physical play with their infants, but there is little question that Aka infants by eight months of age were attached to their fathers. Fathers, for instance, were more likely than mothers to pick up the infant in response to infant desire (an attachment behavior). Whether infants are more attached to their mothers than their fathers is a difficult question. If one uses traditional behaviors to measure attachment (fussing, approaching), mothers are favored because infants frequently demonstrate these behaviors to mothers in order to nurse. But the Aka father receives proportionately more attachment behaviors if one considers the amount of time he holds and is within proximity of the infant. Mothers on average held and were within proximity of their infants more than three times as frequently as fathers, but mothers only received twice as many attachment behaviors as fathers. Aka children also appear to be socially competent, however one may measure this, even though fathers do not play vigorously with them.

The Parsons and Bales (1955) paradigm suggests that fathers also foster social competence by being more punitive and restrictive. Interview data from American adolescents confirm Parsons and Bales expectation (Bronfenbrenner 1961; Kagan and Lempkin 1960). American fathers were seen as disciplinarians while mothers were seen as nurturers. Interviews with sixteen Aka adolescents, on the other hand, run counter to this expectation: Aka adolescents suggest it is the mother rather than the father who is more punitive. Twelve of the sixteen said their mothers most often hit (by slap) them, usually for not doing something they were asked to do, while only two said their fathers. Ten of sixteen said their mothers yelled at them most often, while only two mentioned their fathers. The adolescent data were consistent with the adult responses. Eight of thirteen adults who mentioned a person that often got angry at them when they were children listed their mothers, only one listed fathers, while three listed grandmothers. The above data on "bad" mothers and fathers indicates a greater concern for mothers hitting children than fathers. In the parental interviews, only two of ten fathers said that they had ever hit their child, while five of ten mothers said they had hit their child. There are some inconsistencies and consistencies between the observational data and interview data. While adolescents claimed to have been slapped and some parents say they have hit their children, I have observed a parent hit a child only once in fifteen years of research. Observations are consistent with the view that mothers are more likely to get angry at their children. I have seen mothers chase their children out of camp with knives, throw rocks and sticks at their children, and yell at them.

Mothers are more likely to get angry at children, in part, because mothers are more likely than fathers to engage in multiple tasks in camp and are in greater need of assistance. They frequently try to persuade older children and adolescents to help fetch water or firewood but usually end up getting angry at them for they often refuse to help. Mothers are also responsible for food distribution and get angry at children who raid the food supply while they are absent.

Aka data do tend to support the characterization of mothers as caregivers (e.g., holding, feeding, cleaning)—mothers held the infants more frequently and longer than fathers or other caretakers, and they were more likely to pick up the infant for caretaking purposes than fathers or others. Interview data also support this view. When asked who does one tell if one is hungry, eight of sixteen adolescents said mother, six said paternal grandmother, and two said stepmother; nobody mentioned turning to father for food. Adults also mentioned turning to mother for food most frequently when they were children: eleven of twenty said they turned to mother, three said mother and father, two said grandmother, two said maternal aunt, one said father, and one said paternal uncle.

Contrary to the Parsons and Bales model, there is no clear support either in the observational or in the interview data that mothers provide more nurturing or emotional support than fathers. When adolescents and adults were asked which relative they felt the most sentiments for, only four of twenty-four mentioned their mother or father. Observational data indicated Aka fathers were affectionate and soothed the infant frequently (see chap. 5). When questioned about whom they turned to for sympathy when they were ill, eight of the sixteen adolescents said their mother was more sympathetic while they were ill, five said their father, and three said both mother and father. Adults mentioned going to mother slightly more often for sympathy when sick as a child: seven of twenty said mother was more sympathetic, seven said mother and father, two said father, and four mentioned other relatives. Both mothers and fathers were concerned when their children became ill. Plate 13 shows a concerned Aka couple with their children who are sick with measles and waiting to see an *nganga*.

The Aka father-infant data are not consistent with the extensive American data. The data do indicate that if fathers are consistently active infant and child caregivers (not just a few months as in the Swedish studies [Lamb et al. 1983]), and if fathers know from early experiences and training how to care for infants and children, then (1) vigorous play may not be necessary to establish attachment, (2) punitive discipline may not be necessary to establish social competence, and (3) mothers need not be the overwhelming providers of emotional support.

RESPONSIBILITY

A responsibility questionnaire was given to twenty adults (ten male, ten female) to try and determine if Aka perceived fathers as the second most important infant caretaker. Direct observations certainly indicated this, but did Aka see it this way? The questionnaire consisted of twenty-five hypothetical situations of infant and child caretaking (see table 13). The informant was asked who is responsible for each given situation. In items 1–11 all family members were available for caretaking; in items 12–17 the mother was not available; and in items 18–25 neither mother nor father was available. The questionnaire results reflected the observational findings; fathers are the preferred caretakers when mothers are busy or unavailable. For items 1–11, mother was listed as the preferred caretaker 73.6 percent of the time; for items 12–17, father was listed as the preferred caretaker 69.2 percent of the time; and, for items 18–25, a grandparent or older sibling was the preferred caretaker 90.6 percent of the time.

FATHER'S ROLE IN CULTURAL TRANSMISSION

Classical anthropological descriptions of fathers' roles usually include the educative functions of fathers (Murdock 1949, Fortes 1938, Stephens 1963), but seldom do anthropological studies provide any specific detail about fathers' educational roles. The cultural transmission questionnaire (table 13) provided detailed information on the degree of fathers' involvement in education, the sorts of skills fathers were most likely to transmit, and the significance of the father in his son's acquisition of skills.

When seventy-two individuals (forty adults, sixteen adolescents, sixteen children) were questioned about how they learned fifty skills ($N = 3,600$ responses), fathers were identified as transmitting the skills 31.6 percent of the time; mothers were identified 34.6 percent of the time; and both parents were mentioned 18.2 percent of the time. Parents, and not all members of the camp as Turnbull (1965b) suggests, are the primary transmitters of cultural knowledge among net hunting Aka Pygmies.

Figure 8 examines skills and knowledge transmitted by mothers and fathers. Mothers were more likely to transmit gathering and infant care skills while fathers were more likely to transmit hunting and dancing skills (Hewlett and Cavalli-Sforza 1986). Food preparation, maintenance (house building), mating (dealing with in-laws), sharing, and special skills (e.g., healing) were transmitted equally by mothers and fathers. The data clearly indicate that fa-

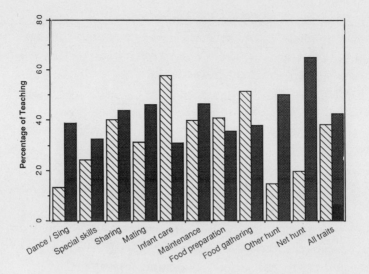

Fig. 8. Percentage of teaching by mothers and fathers

thers, as well as mothers, transmit a broad range of cultural skills and knowledge to their children.

Table 35 shows how a father's role as educator changes with the age of his children. Fathers contributed more skills as their children got older, while mothers contributed the most skills while their children were young. Overall, children learned productive skills by age ten and began to acquire reproductive skills after that age.

Table 36 compares cases for which the mother or father was cited as the educator and indicates a strong relationship between sex of the skilled individual and sex of the teacher: Fathers generally transmitted skills to sons and mothers transmitted skills to daughters. About one of six girls learned primarily from her father.

These data exemplify the high father saliency identified in the behavioral observations. Fathers must be near their children to transmit a substantial percentage of skills to them. Fathers are especially important in transmitting knowledge about hunting and dancing.

116

TABLE 35.   Age Effects on Division of Teaching Labor

Percentage of Skills	Children	Adolescents	Adults
Taught by Father	25.6	37.3	35.3
Taught by Mother	42.8	37.0	31.1

TABLE 36.   Sex of Educator/Sex of Skilled Individual Interactions for Aka of All Ages ($N = 72$) That Were Instructed by Mother or Father (Correlations of 2 $\times$ 2 Tables and Their Significance by χ^2)

Trait Cluster	Percentage Males Taught by		Percentage Females Taught by		χ^2
	Mother	Father	Mother	Father	
All traits	25.7	74.3	83.5	16.5	23.97*
Net hunt	1.6	98.4	67.2	32.8	39.42*
Other hunt	2.0	98.0	80.0	20.0	59.18*
Food gathering	49.0	51.0	85.0	15.0	10.49*
Food prep.	21.3	78.7	87.1	12.9	31.58*
Maintenance	14.9	85.1	89.1	10.9	39.82*
Infant care	49.5	51.5	91.9	8.1	16.25*
Mating	3.0	97.0	86.4	13.6	51.84*
Sharing	27.1	72.9	87.3	12.7	26.67*
Spec. skills	9.1	90.9	39.6	60.4	8.91*
Dance/sing	1.7	98.3	75.0	25.0	45.18*

*$p < .001$ (1 df)

FIVE YEARS LATER: THE IMPORTANCE OF STEPFATHERS AND STEPMOTHERS

I usually return to Bokoka every year, if only for a few weeks, to see how everyone is doing. I have tried to keep in touch with members of the fifteen families who participated in this study since 1984. Changes within the families have been dramatic over the last five years. Four of the original fifteen infants died during this period. Two of those infants had high involvement fathers while the other two had relatively low involvement fathers. Although the data are few, they do suggest that father involvement in itself does not increase or decrease infant or early childhood survival. This was not surprising as fathers contribute to their infants in many ways besides caregiving; providing, educating, and protecting are a few other ways in which Aka fathers contribute to their infants. One pattern is certain when considering the father's role and infant survival—if a father is not identified for the infant, it is unlikely that the infant will live very long. I have recorded three such cases, and the infants all died before their first birthday. Others helped the single mothers, but the mothers seemed to distance themselves from the infants and benignly neglect them. Two of the four infants' deaths were also somewhat linked to dramatic changes in their fathers' roles. One infant died within months after the mother and father divorced, and one child died shortly after the father took a second wife. When the father takes a second wife, he must provide bride service and live with the second wife's family for some time. His first wife and their children do not go with him; they stay with either her husband's or her own family's clan and camp.

While I was previously familiar with the high incidence of infant and child mortality, I was relatively unaware of the importance of stepparenting in the community until I closely followed the fifteen families in this study. During the five-year period there were four divorces, one father was killed by a villager deep in the Congo, and one mother died in the birth of her next child. Six of the original fifteen infants (40 percent) had lost one parent within the first few years of their lives. Of the eleven remaining children today, five live with one parent or a stepparent. One lives with a single father, one lives with a single mother, two have stepfathers, and one has a stepmother.

Like other anthropologists, I tended to neglect the role of stepfathers during the study period. Some observational and interview data were collected on stepfathers and will be mentioned only briefly. The significance of and tremendous need for a study of stepfathers/parents are demonstrated in table 37. A thirteen-year-old Aka child has less than a 60 percent chance of living with both natural parents, and an eighteen-year-old has less than a 30 percent

Pl. 1. Aka father affectionately holding his infant

Pl. 2. Aka net hunters

Pl. 3. Aka woman with infant and basket assists in setting up the family net

Pl. 4. A young Aka girl captures a small duiker in the family net

Pl. 5. A young Aka couple out on a
trail together on their way to a dance

Pl. 6. An Aka father transports his
infant and hunting net

Pl. 7. An Aka father holding his infant during a rest period on the net hunt

Pl. 8. An Aka mother rests with her infant before the hunt begins

Pl. 9. An Aka father stays with
his daughter while his wife
collects firewood

Pl. 10. Aka children with their
father in camp

Pl. 11. An Aka father sings to his daughter late in the evening

Pl. 12. An Aka father and infant that were engaged in face-to-face play

Pl. 13. An Aka couple with their sick children during a major measles epidemic

Pl. 14. Both young and old fathers are involved with their infants. This elderly father holds his infant in camp while mother is out visiting.

Pl. 15. Husband-wife cooperation is extensive. This couple is returning from a net hunt.

Pl. 16. Aka fathers hold their infants in many contexts. This father is out with other men looking for palm wine.

Pl. 17. Ngandu men extrinsically value infant care. This picture symbolizes his desire to be a good provider and have many children. Seldom does he participate in infant care.

chance of living with both natural parents if he or she is not yet married. Death and divorce lead to the high rates of stepparenting. The interview data were consistent with table 37. Thirteen of twenty adults interviewed about their feelings and experiences with their parents had at least one parent die while they were young. Of the thirteen that lost a parent, six lost their mother, three lost their father, and four lost their mother and father. Only two of the twenty adults still had both parents living. As Chagnon (1982) has indicated, the "decay" of the family is not unique to modern industrialized nations; it occurs naturally in traditional societies because of high mortality and divorce rates.

Table 37 describes some other interesting features of Aka stepfathers: (1) almost 25 percent of the sixteen to twenty year olds who have not married live with their father and stepmother; (2) children rarely live only with their fathers (no stepmother) and, (3) although the percentage is small, just as many young children live with their father and stepmother as their mother and stepfather.

The few behavioral observations of stepfathers were inconsistent with the kinds of things Aka adults and adolescents were telling me about stepfathers. Behavioral observations indicated that stepfathers did almost no infant or childcare and were much more likely than a natural father to be idle or away from camp. But stepfather all-day focal observations were few ($N = 3$). In contrast, Aka gave quite positive accounts of their relationships with their stepfathers.

TABLE 37. Percentage of Aka Children That Live with Natural Parents and Stepparents

Percent Coresident with	Age of Child			
	0–5 ($N = 74$)	6–10 ($N = 65$)	11–15 ($N = 33$)	16–20 ($N = 21$)
Mother and father	82.4	73.8	57.6	28.6
Mother and stepfather	2.7	9.2	18.2	19.0
Father and stepmother	2.7	4.6	6.1	23.8
Mother only	12.2	12.4	15.1	23.8
Father only	0.0	0.0	3.0	4.8

All adults interviewed who had stepfathers ($N = 8$) said they had a close relationship, that the stepfathers treated them as their own, and that there were no major problems. Although rare, some informants even said that their stepfather treated them better than anyone else. The only evidence in the interview data of stepfather difficulties came from two (of eight) female adolescents who said that their stepfathers got angry at them more often than anyone else (the other six said it was their mothers). The stepfather data are few and very inconclusive, but the demographics of table 37 suggest that extensive research is needed.

The "emic" data described in this chapter generally reflect the "etic" data from chapters 4 and 5: Aka actions and expressions are both inconsistent with Western models of the father's role. Aka fathers are *not* their infants' vigorous playmates but, in contrast, are nurturing and affectionate and intrinsically enjoy being with their infants. The last three chapters have quantitatively and qualitatively described the Aka father-infant relationship. The next chapter places Aka fathers in cross-cultural perspective and considers social, environmental, and ideological variables that may help explain why Aka fathers are especially intimate. It has been demonstrated that Aka fathers are different from American fathers, but how do they compare to fathers in other non-Western populations and what factors influence the diversity of fathers' roles?

CHAPTER 7

Intracultural and Intercultural Variation in the Father-Infant Relationship

This chapter examines factors that influence intracultural and intercultural variability in fathers' level of involvement and style of care. Theoretical perspectives that identify factors associated with variability in fathers' roles are reviewed and applied to Aka fathers.

VARIABILITY IN THE LEVEL OF FATHER INVOLVEMENT

In attempting to explain the level of father involvement, theorists have generally focused on one or more of three distinct questions: Why do fathers do less direct childcare than mothers? Why do fathers in some cultures do more than fathers in other cultures? And, why do some fathers within a particular culture do more or less childcare than other fathers within that culture? The first question aims at identifying factors associated with the sexual division of labor, while the second and third questions are concerned with factors that explain intercultural and intracultural variability in the level of father involvement.

Why do fathers do less direct childcare than mothers? There is no human society known to man where males do more childcare than females. Evolutionary biologists (Darwin 1871; Bateman 1948; Trivers 1972) explain that like most other mammals, it is a matter of reproductive biology. Human females produce few and therefore costly eggs while males produce millions of relatively inexpensive sperm. Females carry the fetus for nine months and are the ones to nurse the infants after parturition. The female also knows she is the natural mother while the father can never be absolutely sure. As a consequence, males and females have different reproductive strategies: Females enhance their reproductive success by investing in the care of the relatively limited number of offspring they produce, and by carefully selecting fathers who will enhance the survival of their offspring; males enhance their reproductive success by not being as selective in finding a mate, and by investing more time in intrasexual competition for status (as a good hunter, warrior, or businessman) rather than in direct care of children. If successful, a man can have many more children than a woman (through polygyny or serial monogamy). Men do risky tasks because they have more to gain reproductively than women if they are successful. In essence, fathers do less caretaking because it does not enhance their reproductive success as it does for mothers.

While the above evolutionary factors are being considered more seriously in the current literature, most anthropologists have relied upon the "babies and brawn" arguments for explaining mothers' greater involvement in childcare (Mukhopadhyay 1983). The first factor suggests that mothers do more childcare because they nurse infants. Nursing constrains the mother's activities, so the father is more likely to undertake subsistence tasks that take him away from the infant, while the mother is more likely to do subsistence activities compatible with childcare (Brown 1970). This hypothesis also explains why men usually do the more risky subsistence tasks—dangerous tasks may jeopardize infant survival. The second factor suggests that the relative strength of males and females is a critical factor in explaining why mothers do more childcare than fathers. Murdock and Provost (1973) argue that males' superior strength and ability to move with quick bursts of energy are the determining factor in sex differences in childcare allocation. Men would then be expected to do the hunting of large game and women would be responsible for gathering and childcare.

Socialization factors have also been suggested to explain why fathers do less childcare than mothers. The socialization or cultural relativist position is best represented by Margaret Mead in her book *Sex and Temperament* (1935). She suggests that masculine and feminine characteristics are not based on biological sex differences or on economic constraints; they reflect the cultural constructs of different societies. Although she uses a psychoanalytic approach, Chodorow (1973) has built upon the socialization hypothesis by suggesting that it is the degree of intimacy a boy has with his own father that will predict the level of father involvement. If a father is a distant identity figure to his son, then the boy is more likely to exhibit hypermasculine behavior and devalue those things that are feminine (this of course includes childcare).

Durkheim (1933) and Parsons and Bales (1955) take a functionalist approach and suggest that the family can be viewed as a self-contained social microcosm and as a subsystem within a more inclusive social order. As a subsystem it needs to maintain its own integrity and order, and, generally, mothers and fathers have functionally different roles within the family: fathers are primarily responsible for the instrumental and executive tasks that relate the family to its larger social environment, while women specialize in meeting expressive needs and routine tasks within the family. This hypothesis does not explain why mothers do childcare tasks; tasks are assigned to enhance the social solidarity of the family; it just so happens that women perform expressive tasks within the family, which include childcare.

Why do fathers in some cultures do more than fathers in other cultures? Evolutionary biologists have explained intercultural variation in the level of father involvement by identifying three critical factors: distribution of females (Emlen and Oring 1977), paternal certainty (Hartung 1985), and possible ontogenetic factors (Draper and Harpending 1982). According to Emlen and Oring (1977), when females are in a concentrated area (a city or village), the fitness benefits associated with male mating efforts (defending food patches, defending and maintaining a mate, and intrasexual competition) may be high in relation to direct paternal care. In situations where females are widely dispersed (hunter-gatherer camps), Emlen and Oring predict less intrasexual competition and greater paternal care.

Paternity certainty is an important factor for evolutionary biologists. Male-female sexual relations in some cultures are relatively permissive. Women may have many lovers, social paternity is important, divorce rates are high, and extramarital sex is common. In such cultures, evolutionary biologists would predict that direct father involvement would be low because the father would have low paternity certainty. In societies where fathers are relatively certain about paternity, they would predictably invest more time in childcare.

Draper and Harpending (1982) suggest that there is a "sensitive period" from one to five years of age, where boys and girls learn a reproductive and parenting strategy. A boy who sees his mother and father together during this sensitive period would learn that a mate is stable and therefore would have a reproductive strategy that focused on providing for his mate and offspring. A boy with low father salience during early childhood would learn that mates are not stable and would develop a reproductive strategy to deal with male-male competition for mates (e.g., verbal abilities). Due to his perception of an unstable relationship as an adult he would be less likely to invest time in childcare. Generally, males in matrifocal female farming societies tend to exhibit reproductive strategies that emphasize the male-male competition and deemphasize childcare.

> Male children born into matrifocal households exhibit at adolescence a complex of aggression, competition, low male parental investment and derogation of females and femininity . . . (while) male children reared in father-present or nuclear households show less interest in competitive dominance with other males and more interest in manipulation of nonhuman aspects of the environment. (255)

Cultural ecologists have implicated two other factors influencing intercultural variability in the level of father involvement: land

124

availability (Goody 1973) and female contribution to subsistence (Katz and Konner 1981). Goody (1973) compares Eurasian cultures with those of sub-Sahara African and suggests that in Eurasian cultures population density is greater, land availability lower, and social stratification greater than in the sub-Saharan cultures. One consequence of these differences is that Eurasian societies usually practiced dowry, which became part of the conjugal fund that the husband controlled. Men in Eurasian societies, Goody suggests, exercised greater control over women's lives, which often meant that men did less childcare.

Katz and Konner's (1981) cross-cultural study found that when women contributed more to subsistence than men, men were more likely to engage in childcare. They suggest that in such cases women would ask them to help with childcare more often.

Social anthropologists have identified three other factors that may predict intercultural variability in the level of father involvement: warfare, level of polygyny in a society (Katz and Konner 1981), and ideology. Katz and Konner found that fathers in societies that practiced warfare were less proximal (physical and emotional proximity) to their children than fathers in societies that did not practice warfare. The level of polygyny is also statistically related to father proximity; fathers in polygynous societies are less proximal to children than fathers in monogamous societies, supposedly because the polygynous father has to divide his time between more children.

Some anthropologists have examined the symbolic nature of fathers within various cultures and have found that certain societies have "earth" fathers in their mythology, while in other societies fathers are more likely to be associated with the "sky" (Coleman 1981). Fathers belonging to the former type are more likely to participate in childcare.

The last question to be considered is: Why do some fathers within a culture do more or less childcare than other fathers within that culture? Anthropological data in this domain are scarce. At a recent international conference on hunter-gatherer studies one social anthropologist went so far to say that it is not the role of anthropolo-

125

gists to explain intracultural variability. While the statement was not received well by the audience, the lack of ethnographic descriptions of intracultural variability reinforces his view.

Carol Ember's (1973) study of the Luo is one of the few anthropological studies to consider intracultural variability in sex roles. She found that in families where there was no older female sibling to help with childcare the older boy in the family was assigned this as well as other "feminine" tasks. These boys were less aggressive and demonstrated more prosocial behaviors than boys assigned "masculine" tasks. While not a longitudinal study, it suggests that task assignment in childhood could be an important variable in predicting intracultural variability in father involvement.

Aka Intracultural Variability in Level of Fathers' Involvement

Overall, Aka fathers are very involved with their infants; 47 percent of the father's day (twenty-four hour period) is spent holding or within an arm's reach (proximity) of his infant. But as table 38 demonstrates, there is remarkable variation between fathers in the level of involvement during daylight hours. One father, for instance, averaged thirteen minutes during the day holding his infant, while another father averaged almost two hours (117 minutes). Some factors have already been identified as influencing the variability of these measures: subsistence context (forest, village, camp, out-of-camp) and the infant's age. Two other factors that may influence individual variability in the degree of father involvement are the father's status and socialization.

Father's status
In comparing fathers who held their infants frequently with fathers who seldom held their infants, a generalized pattern of traits emerged. High involvement fathers tended to have the following traits: no brothers, few relatives in general, wife from a distant clan, married relatively late in life, monogamous, a small hunting net, more reliant on individual hunting techniques (small traps), and a

close relationship with Ngandu villagers. Moreover, these fathers and their own fathers never held positions of status (*kombeti, tuma* or *nganga*). Aka fathers who seldom held their infants tended to have the opposite characteristics (table 39).

With the small sample size, it is difficult to determine which factor(s) is more important. Table 40 examines some factors that have previously been identified in predicting the level of paternal involvement and demonstrates the age of the father (see pl. 14), sex of the infant, birth order, family composition, and age of the infant are not good predictors of Aka fathers' level of involvement. Statistically significant differences are found between fathers who have many brothers and those who have none, and fathers who are polygynous versus fathers who are monogamous. There is some indication that the number of brothers is slightly more important

TABLE 38. Variability in Degree of Father Involvement Measures

Father Number	Mean Percentage of Time			
	Holding	Within Proximity	Available	Nearest Neighbor
1	5.6	2.4	71.5	19.0
2	7.1	2.0	67.3	12.2
3	14.8	16.7	38.8	16.7
4	16.3	1.1	100.0	30.4
5	6.3	1.0	80.3	6.1
6	5.7	11.4	32.7	2.9
7	15.5	8.1	92.2	24.5
8	16.1	16.3	40.8	18.4
9	1.8	0.0	83.3	23.7
10	5.9	4.1	81.4	16.3
11	5.5	9.8	57.1	12.2
12	3.5	13.6	85.4	27.5
13	6.0	3.4	90.8	29.3
14	1.9	3.8	46.9	17.9
15	6.2	19.6	61.3	21.1
Overall Mean	7.9	7.5	68.6	18.5
SD	5.1	6.6	21.5	8.0

than polygyny. There is little difference, for instance, between the two monogamous fathers with two brothers and the two polygynous fathers with two brothers; the two brothers that are monogamous spent an average of forty-two minutes holding their infants and the two brothers who are polygynous spent thirty-eight minutes holding their infants. The number of brothers is important because the patri-clan forms the core of the hunting-collecting unit. If a male has some brothers he is more likely than a male with no brothers to have a reliable economic unit. Females prefer to marry into a more economically reliable group so they seek males who have more brothers. Consequently, males with brothers do not have to travel

TABLE 39. Mean Number of Minutes Fathers Held Focal Infant and Some Cultural and Demographic Variables

Minutes Held	Infant Age[a]	Number of Brothers	Number of Sisters	Number of Living Parents	Number of Wives	Status of[b] Father	Wife[c] from Trail	Size[d] Net
40.4	1	2	2	1	1	—	Yes	L
51.2	1	2	1	2	2	K	Yes	L
106.7	1	1	1	1	1	—	No	S
117.5	1	0	1	1	1	—	No	S
45.4	1	1	1	2	1	—	No	B
41.1	1	0.5	0.5	1	1	—	Yes	M
111.8	2	0	0	0	1	—	No	S
116.1	2	0	1	0	1	—	No	M
13.0	2	2	2.5	1	2	K	Yes	L
42.5	2	0	0	0	1	—	No	S
39.7	2	0.5	1	1	1	—	No	M
25.2	3	1	2	2	1	K	Yes	L
43.3	3	1	3	1	1	—	Yes	L
13.7	3	1	1	1	2	K	Yes	L
44.7	3	2	1	2	1	K	Yes	M

[a]1 = 1–4 months
 2 = 8–12 months
 3 = 13–18 months
[b]K = *kombeti*
[c]Yes = Wife came from Aka clan that resides near same forest trail to village as husband
 No = Wife came from Aka clan that resides some distance from primary trail
[d]S = Small (less than 30 meters long)
 M = Medium (31–60 meters long)
 L = Large (Greater than 60 meters long)
 B = Bride service (no net of own being used)

as far to find spouses and can marry earlier as more females are attracted to them. This in turn means that the family of the wife is nearby to help support the male's family. Since the father who holds his infant frequently does not have a group of brothers to rely on for cooperation on the net hunt, he relies more on individual or

TABLE 40. Father-holding and Some Demographic and Life Cycle Variables

Variable	N^a	Mean[b]	SD	SE	t
Marriage type					
Monogamy	12	68.4	36.0	10.8	
Polygyny	3	26.0	21.6	15.1	2.1*
No. of father's brothers					
None	4	97.0	36.3	21.0	
Two	4	37.3	16.8	9.7	2.6*
One (or half brother)	7	44.7	29.5	13.2	0.4
Infant birth order					
Firstborn	7	71.1	40.2	16.6	
Later born	8	44.1	30.6	11.5	1.3
Household composition					
Parents & infant only	7	73.4	37.4	15.8	
Parents, infant & sibling(s)	8	41.8	31.0	11.5	1.6
Father's age					
Under 30	7	72.0	39.2	16.1	
Over 30	8	43.2	30.4	11.5	1.4
Sex of infant					
Female	8	58.7	33.8	13.0	
Male	7	54.7	42.5	17.3	0.1
Age of infant (months)					
1–4	6	67.0	35.3	15.8	
8–12	5	64.8	46.1	23.0	0.1
12–18	4	31.7	15.1	8.6	1.3

[a] number of fathers
[b] Mean scores are the average number of minutes fathers spent holding their infant during daylight hours (6 A.M. to 6 P.M.).
*$p < .01$

small group hunting techniques and is more likely to provide labor to Ngandu farmers. The closer tie to Ngandu farmers was quantitatively demonstrated in table 26: Fathers residing in the village who held their infants frequently did twice as much labor for villagers than fathers who did significantly less infant holding.

The data suggest that higher status fathers, that is, fathers with more "kinship resources" (brothers), invest less time in the direct care of their infants. A high status male is one who has many brothers, two wives, and a father who was a *tuma* or *kombeti*. Indirect evidence exists to suggest that fathers with more brothers are of higher status and have in fact more material resources. First, of the seven *kombeti* in the study area for which reliable genealogical data exist, all had at least two full brothers. Second, higher status Aka males (those in position of *kombeti*) had significantly fewer caries than males of the same age (Walker and Hewlett 1990), suggesting that they had a diet higher in protein and fat. The better diet may also explain why the *kombeti* are on average 3 cm taller than the average adult Aka. One might infer that their children may also have a better diet as a consequence of having a higher status father. Third, as demonstrated earlier, the *kombeti* generally has more than one wife and more children, a possible sign that he has more resources. This does not mean that the father who does not hold the infant contributes less; he provides different types of investment (see chaps. 1 and 8). The time that involved fathers spend with their infants, less active fathers may spend talking with other males so as to maintain their status. This status maintenance "indirectly" benefits the infant. Fathers with fewer resources (brothers) compensate by spending more time in the direct care of their infant.

There is some evidence to support the above proposition. It has already been demonstrated that fathers who held their infants less generally had more resources (table 40) and greater status (table 39). Fathers who held less frequently were also observed spending more time talking with others (table 27) than fathers who held their infants frequently. Nearest neighbor data also indicate that fathers who held their infant less were significantly more likely to have other adult males as their nearest neighbor than fathers who held their infants frequently (54.2 percent for the former versus 38.5 percent for the latter ($\chi^2 = 10.7$, $p < .005$ [1 df]). The fact that less involved/higher status fathers talk more often to other adult males suggests that they spend more time in the promotion and maintenance of status rather than in the direct care of their infant. Fathers who have fewer resources available to maintain greater status prefer to spend more time in the direct care of their infants.

An alternative explanation could be proposed. Fathers who have more resources (brothers) and consequently greater status may spend less time caretaking and more time talking to other adult males simply because they have more male relatives to talk to. Lower investing fathers have fewer relatives and therefore would need less time to visit. Indirect evidence from nearest neighbor observations does not support this hypothesis. When an adult male was observed to be the nearest neighbor to a low investing father, 72.7 percent of the nearest neighbor adult males were unrelated (affinal relations were considered unrelated). If the above alternative hypothesis is correct, low investing fathers should be near and talking with brothers or other related adult males, but this is not the case.

Socialization

Another factor that may help explain the intracultural variability in direct father-infant care is the socialization of the father. Do fathers who actively participate in childcare produce sons that become fathers like themselves? The cultural transmission study conducted during the field study (Hewlett and Cavalli-Sforza 1986) and described briefly in chapter 3 demonstrated that Aka culture is transmitted primarily from parent to child. According to a cultural transmission model developed by Cavalli-Sforza and Feldman (1981), this form of transmission predicts great intracultural variability— precisely what we find in Aka paternal involvement. Unfortunately, empirical longitudinal data to test the model (to determine if the highly involved fathers in this study have sons that also become

131

highly involved fathers) do not exist, but some indirect evidence from the cultural transmission interview data might be used to examine the hypothesis. Six of the fifteen focal fathers also participated in the cultural transmission study. Three of these fathers were highly involved (i.e., held their infant over 1 hour and 45 minutes during the 12-hour observation period), and three were less involved (held their infant less than 45 minutes during the 12-hour observation period). As with everyone else in the study, the fathers were asked how they learned each of fifty skills (see table 14). One might use the number of the fifty items that the father indicated his own father taught him, as a measure of the level of involvement of the father's father. The assumption here is that the more skills the father's father transmitted, the greater the level of his direct childcare. The cultural transmission hypothesis would predict that the highly involved fathers would learn more skills from their own fathers than the less involved fathers. Results indicate a pattern just the opposite of what is expected: Highly involved fathers learned 39.3 percent of the fifty skills from their own fathers, while the less involved fathers learned 52 percent of the skills from their fathers. The difference is significant ($\chi^2 = 4.85$, $p < .05$ [1 df]). Ten of the fifty skills questioned were childcare skills. These skills, more than the others, may give a better indication of the level of the involvement of the father's father. The assumption here is that if a father is transmitting childcare skills to his son, he knows these skills well because he is or has been an active infant caretaker. But, as with the fifty skills, more childcare skills were reported to be transmitted by less involved fathers: Less involved fathers learned 33.3 percent of the childcare skills from their fathers while involved fathers learned only 13.3 percent of the childcare skills from their fathers.

Without family histories of each of the focal fathers, it would be difficult to make sense of the above cultural transmission data. The family histories indicate that the three fathers who learned many items from their own fathers but did less direct childcare with their own children had fathers who were around until they married. The fathers who learned few items from their own fathers but did substantially more direct caretaking with their own children had stepfathers at a very early age (four to five years old). The number of skills transmitted by a father appears to be a function of the number of years the father was present to consistently instruct and provide a model for the son, rather than the amount of time the father participated in childcare.

Ember's (1973) study of the Luo may be useful for understanding Aka intracultural variability. Luo boys who had no sisters to help with childcare were given some "feminine" task assignments and as a consequence were more likely to be less aggressive and to demonstrate prosocial behaviors. Family composition and task assignment may be influential factors in predicting Aka father involvement. Observational data indicate that Aka stepfathers are less involved with stepchildren than with their natural children. If a boy is living with his stepfather, he may be called upon by his mother to help in the childcare of his full brothers and/or sisters because his stepfather provides infrequent care of the stepchildren. This suggests that Aka boys with stepfathers are more likely to be given "feminine tasks" than Aka boys who live with their natural parents. Consequently, they would more likely be nurturing adults and participate in their own infants' care. It is not possible to test this hypothesis with existing data. The most involved Aka fathers did live with stepfathers at an early age, but it is not known if they were called upon more often than other boys to help in childcare or other "feminine" tasks.

Aka Fathers' Level of Involvement in Cross-Cultural Perspective

Aka father involvement is exceptional, if not unique, by cross-cultural standards. Tables 41 and 42 place Aka fathers' holding and availability in a cross-cultural context. Aka fathers hold their infants and are around their children more than twice as often as fathers in other societies where comparable data exist. Why do Aka fathers do so much more caregiving than fathers in other societies? What factors influence the variability demonstrated in tables 41 and 42?

133

Like many other foragers, the Aka have few accumulable resources that are essential for survival. Males essentially inherit a
most important resource, brothers. Aka males and females also
contribute a similar percentage of calories to the diet. In societies
unlike the Aka, where resources essential to survival can be accumulated or where males are the primary contributors to subsistence,
evolutionary biologists would predict that fathers would invest more
time competing for these resources and, consequently, less time
with their children. In contrast, where resources are not accumulable or men are not the primary contributors to subsistence, men
generally would spend more time in the direct care of their children.

TABLE 41. Comparison of Father-Holding in Selected Foraging and Farming
Populations

Population	Age of Infants (in months)	Subsistence	Father Holding (% of time)	Source
Gidgingali (Australia)	0–6 6–18	Settled foragers	3.4 3.1	Hamilton 1981
!Kung (Africa)	0–6 6–24	Foragers	1.9 4.0	West and Konner 1976
Efe Pygmies (Africa)	1–4	Foragers	2.6	Winn, Morelli, and Tronick 1990
Aka Pygmies (Africa)	1–4 8–18	Foragers	22.0 14.0	Chapter 4
Black Carib (Belize)	3–18	Farmers	0.0	Munroe and Munroe 1989
Logoli (Africa)	3–18	Farmers	0.0	Munroe and Munroe 1989
Newars (India)	3–18	Farmers	2.0	Munroe and Munroe 1989
Samoans	3–18	Farmers	0.0	Munroe and Munroe 1989

Note: All observations were made in the camp or house/yard.

Holocultural and field studies tend to support this hypothesis. Katz and Konner (1981:174) found that father-infant proximity (degree of emotional warmth and physical proximity) is closest in gathering-hunting populations (gathered foods by females are principal resources, meat is secondary) and most distant in cultures where herding or advanced agriculture is practiced. In the latter cultures, cattle, camels, and land are considered the essential accumulable resources for survival. These findings are consistent with Whiting and Whiting's (1975) holocultural study of husband-wife intimacy. They found husband-wife intimacy to be greatest in cultures without accumulated resources or capital investments. While there are other factors to consider (the protection of resources and polygyny rate), there is a strong tendency for fathers/husbands to devote more time to their children/wives if there are no accumulable resources. Table 41 supports the holocultural findings that fathers in societies with

ABLE 42.   Comparison of Father Presence with Infants or Children among Selected Foraging
d Farming Populations

ɔpulation	Location	Subsistence	% Time Father Present/in View	Primary Setting of Observations	Source
usii	Kenya	Farming	10	House/yard and garden	1
Iixteca	Mexico	Farming	9	House/yard	1
ɔcano	Philippines	Farming	14	House/yard	1
kinawan	Japan	Farming	3	Public placès and House/yard	1
ajput	India	Farming	3	House/yard	1
Kung	Botswana	Foraging	30	Camp	2
ka Pygmies	Central African Republic	Foraging	88	Forest camp	3
ogoli	Kenya	Farming	5	House/yard	4
ʻewars	Nepal	Farming	7	House/yard	4
amoans	Samoa	Farming	8	House/yard	4
lack Carib	Belize	Farming	3	House/yard	4
aluk	Micronesia	Farming-fishing	13	House/yard	5

Sources: 1. Whiting and Whiting 1975; 2. West and Konner 1976; 3. chapter 4; 4. Munroe and Munroe 1989;
    5. Betzig, Harrigan, and Turke 1990.

accumulable resources are less likely to spend time near children than fathers in societies where there are few accumulable resources and where men contribute less to the diet than females.

Katz and Konner also found that in societies where hunting by men was the primary mode of subsistence (hunter-gatherers not gatherer-hunters), father-infant proximity was distant. This is consistent with recent field studies conducted among Ache foragers. Meat and honey collected by Ache men represent the majority of calories consumed (Hill and Kaplan 1988), and Ache fathers hold their children on average only ten minutes per day (Hill et al., 1985). This is the lowest amount of paternal holding recorded for a foraging population that has been quantitatively investigated; no other population where males contribute the majority of subsistence foods has been intensively investigated.

While the above hypothesis correctly predicts differences between intensive farmers and gatherers, and between hunter-gatherers and gatherer-hunters, it is not useful for predicting intercultural variability among foraging populations where females contribute significantly to the diet (gatherer-hunters, such as Efe Pygmies of Zaire and !Kung of the Kalahari). Table 42 demonstrates some of the variability in direct paternal care of infants in societies that have been quantitatively investigated and where females contribute significantly to the diet. Among the Efe and !Kung, females contribute substantially more calories than males (Lee 1979; Peacock 1985), whereas Aka men and women contribute nearly equal amounts. Men in all three societies are not responsible for the majority of the calories consumed and there are no accumulable resources essential for survival. Consequently, these fathers may have more time to invest in the direct care of infants than the Ache fathers. Females in these populations would also benefit by selecting males who would be willing and capable of doing childcare since women are less dependent on men for subsistence. But if the above hypothesis were sensitive to intra-gatherer variation, it would predict that Aka fathers should spend less time with infants than is indicated, since Aka men contribute more to subsistence than Efe or !Kung fathers (Aka males contribute 50 percent of calories to diet, Efe males 35 percent, and !Kung males 30 percent).

The comparative data call into question another factor that is often cited when predicting the level of father involvement: female contribution to subsistence (Katz and Konner 1981). If mothers are busy and contribute the essential resources to the diet, this hypothesis predicts that they would call on fathers to help in childcare. Again, if this were so, Efe and !Kung mothers should be getting more infant care from their husbands than Aka mothers.

Other factors often cited as influencing the level of paternal involvement are not useful in explaining intracultural variability among foragers where females contribute the majority of the resources. Paternity certainty, sex-ratio, and level of polygyny are important factors for evolutionary biologists and cultural anthropologists but they do not help explain why Aka fathers do substantially more direct caretaking than Efe or !Kung fathers. Based on blood analysis, paternity certainty is known to be high for both !Kung and Aka, therefore it is not helpful in explaining differences in paternal care between these two groups. The sex-ratio for individuals over fifteen years of age is 0.86 for !Kung (Lee 1979:48), 1.10 for Efe (Bailey and Peacock 1988), and 0.90 for Aka. Evolutionary biologists might suggest that if there are many more adult males than adult females, such as among the Yanomamö, then male-male competition for females would be greater and males would contribute less to the direct care of infants. But the Efe have the greatest male-to-female ratio, and yet they do just as much infant holding as !Kung. Consequently, sex-ratios are not useful for understanding paternal involvement.

Level of polygyny is also considered an important factor in predicting the level of father involvement. In societies where levels of polygyny are high, direct care by fathers is predicted to be low because male-male competition is expected to be higher, and polygynous fathers must divide their time among more children. But the Efe and !Kung levels of polygyny are much lower than the Aka (3–4 percent among Efe and !Kung versus 15 percent among the Aka); paternal infant care patterns should be just the opposite of those found.

One demographic factor that is related to the level of paternal involvement in these three foraging populations is the total fertility rate (TFR). Efe live in an infertility belt in northeastern Zaire and women average only 2.6 live births during their lifetime (Bailey 1989). !Kung women average 4.7 live births (Howell 1979) and Bokoka Aka women average 6.2 live births. The TFR cline follows the paternal involvement cline: The Efe have the lowest fertility and level of paternal involvement, the !Kung are intermediate in both, and the Aka are highest in both measures. Bailey (1985:185) states that "strong father-child attachments among the Efe were uncommon . . . while fathers took on the responsibility of disciplining their children, they were no more likely to care for their children than most other men in camp." Peacock's (1985) behavioral observations indicate that Efe grandmothers, subadult women, old women, and infertile women contribute to infant care, but she does not mention fathers. The low level of Efe paternal involvement may be, in part, due to the availability of other adult females to assist with caregiving. Aka fathers are on the high end, in part, because there are few other adult women without children to help out. But as will be discussed below, fertility is only one contributing factor to high Aka father involvement.

Three factors seem to be especially influential in understanding the extraordinarily high level of Aka paternal care. First, the nature of Aka subsistence activity is rather unique cross-culturally. Usually men's and women's subsistence activities take place at very different locations. The net hunt and other subsistence activities, such as caterpillar collecting, involve men, women, and children. If men are going to help with infant care on a regular basis, they have to be near the infant a good part of the day. The net hunt makes this possible. The net hunt also requires that men and women walk equal distances during the day. In most foraging societies, females do not travel as far from camp as males. Older siblings are not useful for helping their mothers because of the extensive labor involved in walking long distances with an infant. If a mother is to receive help on the net hunt, it needs to come from an adult. Most of the other adult females carry baskets full of food and have their own infants or young children to carry since fertility is high. Fathers are among the few alternative caregivers regularly available on the net hunt to help mothers.

While fathers do carry infants on the net hunt, especially on the return from the hunt when the mothers' baskets are full of meat, collected nuts, and fruit, father-infant caregiving is much more likely to occur in the camp. Aka fathers' behavior in camp does not appear to be ecologically "adaptive" as it does on the forest net hunt. Two other factors need to be considered: the husband-wife relationship and father-infant attachment. The net hunt dramatically influences the husband-wife relationship. The net hunt contributes to the time husband and wife spend together and patterns that time. A husband and wife are together much of the time. Behavioral observations in the forest and village indicated that husbands and wives are within sight of each other 46.5 percent of daylight hours. This is more time together than in any other known society, and it is primarily a result of the net hunt. This percentage of course increases in the evening hours. But, husbands and wives are not only together most of the day, they are actively cooperating on the net hunt. They have to know each other well to communicate and cooperate throughout the day. They work together to set up the family net, chase game into the net, butcher and divide the game, and take care of the children. Husbands and wives help each other out in a number of domains, in part because they spend so much time together (see pl. 15). Husband-wife relations are multistranded. Multistranded reciprocity is an important component of the husband-wife relationship. When they return to camp the mother has a number of tasks—she collects firewood and water and prepares the biggest meal of the day. The father has relatively few tasks to do after returning from the hunt. He may make string or repair the net, but he is available to help with infant care. He is willing to do infant care, in part, because of the multistranded reciprocity between husband and wife (see chap. 2 for a more detailed description of gender relations). In many societies men have fewer tasks to do at the end of the day, while women have domestic tasks and prepare a meal. Men are available to help out with childcare but seldom provide much assistance. Ngandu fathers, for instance, are around the house in the evening, but mothers continue to hold the infants as they collect firewood and prepare the meal.

The third important factor in understanding Aka fathers' involvement with infants is father-infant attachment. Father and infant are clearly attached to each other as evidenced by their frequent interaction. Fathers end up holding their infants frequently because the infants crawl to them. Fathers pick up their infants because they intrinsically enjoy infants. Figure 6 clearly demonstrates that infants seek out their fathers. Fathers are also attached to their infants. They enjoy being with them and carry them in a number of different contexts (out in the fields drinking palm wine with other males).

While these three factors are especially influential, other factors also play a part: near equal contributions to the diet by males and females; relatively high fertility rates; lack of warfare and violence, especially against women and children; a fierce egalitarian ethic; a mobile foraging lifestyle where it is not useful to accumulate material goods.

Aka fathers and their cultural patterns are unique in the cross-cultural record. Multiple factors have been identified that influence the nature of father-infant relations cross-culturally. Only one common pattern emerges from this overview of intracultural and intercultural variability in father involvement: generally, men will spend more time with their children when they have fewer resources to offer. An important way in which men may compete for a wife is by accrual/expenditure of parental resources. Intraculturally, Aka fathers with more brothers have more resources available to them and, consequently, spend more time in activities such as status maintenance than in direct child care. Aka fathers with no brothers and few resources spend considerably more time in the direct care of children. Interculturally, men in societies in which men accumulate essential resources (land or cattle) or contribute the majority of calories to the diet spend significantly less time in the direct care of children than men in societies where males contribute less to the diet than females. Fathers in these societies have fewer resources to offer and therefore have more time to invest in the survival of their children. It is also to the females' advantage in such societies to select men who demonstrate the desire and ability to do direct childcare.

VARIABILITY IN FATHERS' STYLE OF INTERACTION

Anthropologists have not paid much attention to the father's style of interaction. Anthropological studies generally assume that if the father is involved with infants and children, he has warm and affectionate interactions with them, while fathers who are not involved in childcare are aloof in their interactions with children. The assumed relationship between involvement and style of interaction can be seen in Barry and Paxson's (1971) cross-cultural code for the "role of father." The father's "proximity" to infants or children is defined as both physical and emotional closeness.

Some British social anthropologists have identified factors that predict intercultural variability in the father's style of interaction with children: inheritance and descent rules. Radcliffe-Brown in his seminal article on mother's brother (1924) initiated the idea that:

> The presence of patrilineal descent groups tends to produce a situation where restraint and authority center about father and the male and female members of his descent group. At the same time, informality and indulgence characterize relations with mother and all of the male and female members of mother's patrilineage. (543)

Thus, in a patrilineal society the mother's brother becomes a male mother and the father's sister becomes a female father. Malinowski

141

(1929) went on to describe how just the opposite occurred in matrilineal societies, such as the Trobriand Islanders. Malinowski characterized Trobriand fathers as very indulgent:

> He (father) will fondle and carry a baby, clean and wash it, and give it the mashed vegetable food. . . . The father performs his duties with genuine natural fondness: he will carry an infant about for hours, looking at it with eyes of such love and pride as are seldom seen in those of a European. (201)

The closeness between father and children exists, according to Malinowski, because family authority rests with males on the mother's side of the family.

Goody (1959) criticized Radcliffe-Brown's hypothesis but modified it only slightly by indicating that it was the system of inheritance that was important, not necessarily the rule of descent.

> It is because the father is not vested with jural authority over his son and the son has no title to the inheritance of his father's properties or to succession to his offices and rank, that matrilineal fathers and sons have an affectionate, noncompetitive relationship. Conversely, it is because maternal uncles have jurally sanctioned rights over their nephews and the latter have jurally sanctioned claims on their uncles that there is tension in their relationship. And the pattern is reversed in patrilineal systems because the locus of rights and claims is jurally reversed. Matrilineal fatherhood is defined as primarily a domestic relationship with only a minimal function in the politico-jural domain. Hence its focus is the task of bringing up and educating a child and fathers must rely on moral and affectional sanctions to fulfill it. (Fortes 1958:12 in discussing Goody's comparison on the LoDagaba and Lowilli father-son relationship)

Schneider (1961) in his analysis of matrilineal kinship systems also lists an affective father-child relationship as a distinctive feature of matrilineal descent groups. A cross-cultural test of the hypothesis indicated significant differences in father-child proximity between matrilineal and patrilineal societies (Hewlett 1977).

Aka Intracultural Variability in Caregiving Style

The Aka data do not support the descent theory hypothesis mentioned above. The Aka are patrilineal, but Aka fathers act like fathers in matrilineal societies—they are indulgent and affectionate.

Just as there is considerable variability in Aka fathers' level of involvement, there is marked variability in Aka fathers' style of caregiving. Table 43 examines two areas—fathers' activities with their infants per hour while holding, and attachments displayed toward fathers per hour. Attachment behaviors demonstrated to fa-

TABLE 43. Intracultural Variation in Frequency of Activities While Holding Infant and Attachment Behaviors

Father Number	Father Age Group[a]	Infant Age Group[b]	Activities[c]	Attachment[d]
1	O	1	1.11	0.0
2	Y	1	4.19	0.0
3	Y	1	14.14	0.0
4	Y	1	6.79	0.0
5	Y	1	3.30	0.0
6	O	1	3.46	0.0
7	O	2	3.30	0.6
8	Y	2	7.43	0.5
9	O	2	4.00	0.5
10	O	2	2.89	1.3
11	O	2	3.67	1.0
12	Y	3	5.00	1.9
13	O	3	0.73	2.6
14	O	3	2.72	3.5
15	Y	3	13.45	2.5

[a]Y is under 30 years of age and O is over 30 years of age.
[b]1 is 1–4 months; 2 is 8–12 months; 3 is 13–18 months.
[c]frequency of father feeding, cleaning, playing (all types), soothing, and affection per hour while holding
[d]frequency of attachment behaviors displayed toward father per hour

thers vary little, if the age of the infant is considered. The number of attachment behaviors toward the father slowly increases as the infant gets older and is able to crawl or walk toward the father (demonstrate attachment behaviors). Marked variability does exist in the frequency that the father engages in activities with the infant while holding. Two fathers were very interactive and engaged in over twelve activities per hour while holding their infants, while two fathers interacted less than two times per hour while holding. A major factor influencing the variability was the age of the father. Younger fathers, on average, engaged in 7.57 activities per hour while holding their infants, while older fathers averaged 2.71 activities per hour while holding. The difference was statistically significant ($\chi^2 = 26.45$, $p < 0.01[1$ df]). When each activity is considered separately, most correlate with age. The frequency of cleaning, playing, soothing, and affection all showed a statistically significant relationship to age, while feeding and transporting did not.

Comparing Aka and American Fathers' Style of Interaction

Aka father data do not support the contention that fathers are the vigorous, rough-and-tumble playmates of the infants as the data for American fathers indicate. They do suggest that, in comparison to mothers, fathers are slightly more playful: fathers are somewhat more likely to engage in minor physical play with their one-to four-month-old infants than are mothers, and fathers play more frequently with infants while holding than mothers do. But characterizing the Aka father as the infant's playmate would be misleading. Other caretakers holding the infant engage in play with the infant much more frequently than fathers or mothers, and mothers have more episodes of play over the course of a day than fathers or other caretakers because they hold the infant most of the time. The Aka father-infant relationship might be better characterized by its intimate and affective nature. It has already been mentioned that Aka fathers hold their infants more than fathers from any other human population known to anthropologists. Aka fathers also show affection more frequently while holding than mothers, and infants seem to regularly seek father-holding, possibly because of its affective nature.

So how can vigorous play be a significant feature in American studies of father-infant attachment, but not among the Aka? Four factors appear to be important for understanding Aka infant play and attachment: familiarity with the infant, knowledge of caretaking practices (how to hold an infant, how to soothe an infant), the degree of relatedness to the infant, and cultural values and parental goals.

First, due to frequent father-holding and availability, Aka fathers know their infants intimately. Fathers know the early signs of infant hunger, fatigue, and illness as well as the limits in their ability to soothe the infant. They also know how to stimulate responses from the infant without being vigorous. Unlike American fathers, Aka wait for infants to initiate interaction. The Aka mother is even more familiar with the infant's cues; other caretakers are least familiar with them. As indicated earlier, these other caretakers play more frequently with the infant while holding than mothers or fathers and are the most physical in their play, suggesting a relationship between intimate knowledge of the infant's cues and the frequency of play while holding.

Second, knowledge of infant caretaking practices seems to play a role in determining how much play is exhibited in caretaker-infant interactions. Child caretakers were the most physical and the loudest (singing) in their handling of infants. Children were not restricted from holding infants, but they were closely watched by parents. While "other" caretakers were more playful than mothers or fathers, younger fathers and "other" caretakers were more physical than older ones probably because they did not know how to handle and care for infants as well as adult caretakers.

A third factor to consider is the degree of relatedness of the caretaker to the infant. If vigorous play can assist in developing attachment, more closely related individuals may have a greater vested interest in establishing this bond than distantly related individuals. Attachment not only enhances the survival of the infant, but it can potentially increase the related caretaker's inclusive fitness (i.e., if the infant survives to reproductive age, the related caretaker will perpetuate some of his or her own genetic composition [called inclusive fitness by evolutionary biologists]). Aka mothers and fathers establish attachment by their frequent caretaking; vigorous play is not necessary to establish affective saliency. Brothers and sisters, on the other hand, might establish this bond through physical play. Aka brothers and sisters, in fact, provided essentially all of the physical play the focal infants received; cousins and unrelated children were more likely to engage in face-to-face play with the infant instead of physical play.

Finally, the general social context of infant development should be considered. American culture encourages individualistic aggressive competition; Aka culture values cooperation, nonaggression, and prestige avoidance (one does not draw attention to oneself even, for instance, if one kills an elephant). Apparently, Americans tolerate—if not actually encourage—aggressive rough-and-tumble types of play with infants. Also, due to the high infant mortality rate, the primary parental goal for Aka is the survival of their infants. The constant holding and immediate attention to fussing reflect this goal. In the United States, infant mortality rates are markedly lower and, as a result, parental concern for survival may not be as great. The Aka infant is taken away from a caretaker who plays roughly with the infant, in part, because it could be seen as aggressive behavior, but also because the pervasive aim of infant care practices is survival of the infant, and rough-and-tumble play could risk the infant's safety.

These factors tentatively clarify why Aka fathers do not engage in vigorous play like American fathers but do participate in slightly more physical play than Aka mothers (but not more than other caretakers). American fathers seldom participate directly in infant care and consequently are not as familiar with infant cues. To stimulate interaction and (possibly) attachment, they engage in physical play. Aka brothers and sisters are also much less physical in their play with infants than American fathers (Aka never tossed infants in the air or swung them by their arms), again suggesting that Aka children know their infant brother or sister and the necessary infant caregiving skills better than American fathers. These observations are obviously speculative and need further empirical study.

Sociologists LaRossa and LaRossa (1981) describe stylistic differences between American mothers' and fathers' interactions with their infants. They list a number of male-female role dichotomies that reflect different parenting styles. One distinction they make is role distance versus role embracement. Fathers are more likely to distance themselves from the parenting role while mothers are more likely to embrace the parenting role. American women generally want to remain in primary control of the children, and while fathers may show interest in caregiving, they are more likely to distance themselves from caregiving while embracing their roles as breadwinners. LaRossa and LaRossa also suggest that fathers generally have low intrinsic value and relatively high extrinsic value, while mothers have the reverse.

> The intrinsic value of something or someone is the amount of sheer pleasure or enjoyment that one gets from experiencing an object or person. The extrinsic value of something or someone is the amount of social rewards (e.g., money, power, prestige) associated with having or being with the object or person. (64)

They use this dichotomy to explain why fathers are more likely to carry or hold an infant in public than in private. Fathers receive extrinsic rewards from those in public settings, while this does not happen in the home. According to LaRossa and LaRossa, fathers

> will roughhouse with their toddlers on the living-room floor, and will blush when hugged or kissed by the one-year-olds, but when you really get down to it, they just do not have that much fun when they are with their children. If they had their druthers, they would be working at the office or drinking at the local pub. (65)

147

These role dichotomies may be useful for understanding American mother-father parenting styles, but they have limited value in characterizing Aka mother-father distinctions. Aka mothers and fathers embrace the parenting role. Generally, mothers and fathers want to hold their infants, and certainly they derive pleasure from infant interactions. As indicated in chapter 5, fathers were in fact more likely to show affection while holding than mothers. Fathers also offered their nipples to infants who wanted to nurse, cleaned mucus from their infants' noses, picked lice from their infants' hair, and cleaned their infants after they urinated or defecated (often on the father). Fathers' caregiving did not appear any more or less perfunctory than mothers'. Aka fathers are not burdened with infant care; if a father does not want to hold or care for the infant he gives the infant to another person. Overall, Aka fathers embrace their parenting role, much as they embrace their hunting role.

The intrinsic-extrinsic role dichotomy does not fit well with Aka mother-father parenting styles either. Again, both Aka mothers and fathers place great intrinsic value and little extrinsic value on parenting. The fathers' intrinsic value is demonstrated above, but the lack of extrinsic value among the Aka can best be seen by comparing Aka and Ngandu fathers (see pls. 16–17). When an Ngandu father holds his infant in public, he is "on stage." He goes out of his way to show his infant to those who pass by and frequently tries to stimulate the infant while holding it. He is much more vigorous in his interaction with the infant than are Aka men. The following experience exemplifies Ngandu fathers' extrinsic value toward their infants. The man in plate 17 showed me a large fish he had just caught and I asked to take a photograph of him with his fish. He said fine, promptly picked up his nearby infant, and proudly displayed both fish and infant. His wife was also nearby but was not invited into the photograph. Aka, on the other hand, are matter-of-fact about their holding or transporting of infants in public places. They do not draw attention to their infants. The Aka also hold their infants in all kinds of social and economic contexts.

This chapter has examined intracultural and intercultural variability in the father-infant relationship and has identified ecological, demographic, social, psychological, and ideological factors that influence this variability. The next chapter takes us beyond father involvement with infants and considers other forms of paternal "investment" over the course of human history.

CHAPTER 8

Fathers' Role in Human Evolution

To this point, the book has focused on fathers' involvement with their infants. This chapter takes us back in time and considers the diversity of fathers' roles over human history by examining the various forms of human male parental investment. As discussed in chapter 1, the term *investment* comes from evolutionary biology and refers to a range of the father's activities and behaviors that contributes to the survival and fitness of his offspring. Father involvement, the primary topic until now, is only one form of male parental investment.

The importance of the various forms of parental investment has varied dramatically over the course of human evolution. Table 44 examines the importance of these various forms of male parental investment since the Late Pleistocene era, a relatively recent segment of human history (the last 120,000 years). Table 45 outlines some features of subsistence, demography, and social organization during this time period that may help explain why some aspects of father investment were considered more important than others in table 44. This brief reconstruction of fathers' roles in human evolution should be considered heuristic and speculative. The reconstruction is based upon archaeological data as well as contemporary ethnographic analogy. Unfortunately, details about the social life of early human populations are not inscribed on the bones and stones that archaeologists uncover. Consequently, once particular subsistence and settlement patterns are determined from the material

TABLE 44. Variability in Fathers' Roles in Human Evolution

Form of Male Investment	Late Pleistocene	Holocene Foragers	Horticult. Collectors	Intensive Farmers	Modern
Direct					
Proximity maintenance	1	1	1	2	3
Economic contributor	1	2	3	1	2
Direct caretaking	3	2	3	3	2
Cultural transmission	1	1	1	1	3
Inheritance	3	3	2	1	1
Indirect					
Kin network	1	1	1	1	3
Defend resources	2	2	1	2	3
Support mother	1	1	2	1	1

Note: 1 = very important; 2 = important; 3 = minimal importance

TABLE 45. Changes in Subsistence, Demography, and Social Organization Since the Late Pleistocene

Features	Late Pleistocene Hunter-Gatherers	Holocene Foragers	Horticulturalists, Collectors	Intensive Agriculture	Modern
Reliance on large game	High	Low	Rare	None	None
Male contribution to diet	Very high	Medium	Low	High	Medium
Fertility/child mortality	High/high	High/high	High/high	Very high/high	Low/low
Social organization	Patrilocal, patrilineal Polygyny	Bilocal, bilateral Monogamy	Unilocal, unilineal Polygyny	Patrilocal, patrilineal Polygyny (elite) Monogamy (peasants)	Neolocal, bilateral Monogam

artifacts, contemporary populations with similar subsistence and settlement patterns are used to reconstruct the social life of the early cultures.

Late Pleistocene hunter-gatherers were of the same species as contemporary humans (*Homo sapiens*) and relied heavily on large game for subsistence. Since only men are known to hunt large game in hunter-gatherer societies today, it is suggested that Late Pleistocene men did the hunting and were important contributors to the family diet. Sexual dimorphism in size was also greater in the Late Pleistocene period (Foley 1986), which among mammals is usually associated with polygamous mating systems. Due to the importance of the male contribution to the diet and the high level of polygyny it is hypothesized that fathers did not do much in the way of direct care since fathers in contemporary populations with similar features provide infrequent direct care of children (Katz and Konner 1981). Fathers probably provided indirect forms of caregiving (watching children) since fathers, mothers, and children probably slept together and because fathers were in and out of camp during the day. Also, since population densities were relatively low, game was abundant, and accumulation was relatively unimportant, fathers were likely to be time-minimizers, that is, once they had enough game for a day or two they stopped hunting. They probably had a lot of leisure time around camp, during which they would be available to their children. Toward the end of the Late Pleistocene, hunter-gatherers had diverse and complex technologies as well as elaborate art forms, which suggests that fathers probably had an important role in the transmission of culture.

With the warming of the earth and the end of the Ice Age about 12,000 years ago, resource availability, distribution, and quality changed (Foley 1986). Three general subsistence patterns slowly emerged around this time—foraging (mobile hunter-gatherers), collecting (sedentary hunter-gatherers), and simple farming (horticulturalists). Foragers adapted to environments, such as the desert, arctic and the tropical forest regions, where resources were stable but widely dispersed. With the exception of the Inuit in the arctic, women became regular contributors to the diet as gathered vegetable foods became important additions to the small-to-medium-sized game captured by the men. Direct caretaking by fathers increased among Holocene foragers because of the increased contributions of the women, the monogamous marriage pattern, and the lack of organized warfare. Contemporary foraging societies that lack warfare, practice monogamy, and use gathering as an important subsistence activity have physically and emotionally close fathers (Katz and Konner 1981). Gathering by men and women, or cooperative hunting, would also increase father's availability to his children. Inheritance was not an important factor in the father's role in the Late Pleistocene period or for Holocene foragers because there was essentially little to inherit from fathers. Land was generally plentiful and not actively defended, and the accumulation of material goods was limited due to the mobility of the people.

Collectors and horticulturalists also emerged during the Holocene. In areas with abundant, clumped, and predictable resources (areas with maritime and riverine resources), sedentary hunter-gatherers (collectors) made a living. Early domestication, on the other hand, seems to have developed in "marginal" or "tension" zones—zones between resource rich areas, which were experiencing population pressures (Binford 1968). As the early farmers became more successful and as their populations increased, they eventually moved into areas with rich soils and regular rainfall. With sedentarization and domestication (collectors and horticulturalists in tables 44–45), the importance of inheritance and protection in the father's role increased. Environmentally rich areas for farming, collecting, or animal grazing could be inherited and had to be defended against raids by mobile hunter-gatherers and others. The inheritance of a salmon fishing territory, land, or cattle could be important to the survival and success of a father's children. Since polygyny and warfare were common among collectors and horticulturalists, it is suggested that direct care of infants and children by fathers was minimal. But horticultural and collector fathers were likely to be around and available to their children since they contributed little to subsistence. Fathers' roles as providers dropped substantially as women did most of the farming and collecting in these populations.

About 5,000 years ago, irrigation, population pressures, and the development of the plow in some environmentally or socially "circumscribed" areas (Carneiro 1970) led to intensive farming and the origin of the state. Where intensive farming exists, men do most of the plowing or fieldwork and are important providers for their families, whereas women do most of the food processing and preparation, and childcare in and around the home. Material wealth and land became even more important at this stage, and, consequently, inheritance became an important form of paternal investment. The father's role as defender and protector probably decreased as warriors or military employed by the state protected and defended the territory and valuable resources.

The last category is called "modern" and refers to contemporary white middle class, dual income families in the United States. Only in modern societies is the father's role as cultural transmitter and provider of a kin network substantially diminished. An extensive education system provides most of the subsistence skills and cultural knowledge necessary for children to make a living, and the state provides for people who do not have family members to help them out. Fathers in nonindustrial populations often say that they want to have many children so each child has a support network in a time of need and can call on other family members if he or she is physically threatened (Burbank and Chisholm 1989). As in other accumulating societies, inheritance can be an important form of father investment. The father's direct caregiving increases at this stage, and his role as provider decreases, since mothers are employed and there are very few children in the family. There is less proximity maintenance by fathers as they are not around their children during the day and do not sleep with them. An indirect form of paternal investment becomes especially pronounced at the modern stage— the emotional support of the mother, especially if she is not employed. Previously, women lived with and conducted activities with other, usually female, relatives and had opportunities throughout

155

the day to discuss feelings and problems. But in modern neolocal societies women are relatively isolated from others and therefore come to rely upon their husbands for emotional support.

There are two major points to this very simplified and hypothetical overview of fathers' roles in the last 120,000 years of human evolution. First, fathers invest or contribute to their children in many ways. Most discussions of fathers' roles in Euroamerican studies (Lamb, Pleck, Charnov, and LeVine 1987) only consider the caretaking and economic roles of fathers. Since most people today live in nation states, fathers are less likely to play an active role in defending territory or natural resources and are less involved in the transmission of culture. The state provides a military to protect and teachers to educate. All forms of father investment can be considered important given particular ecological, demographic, and social contexts. As environments, technologies, and ideologies have changed, fathers (as well as other members of the family) have adapted in different ways. Today, direct caretaking and the emotional support of the mother are seen as increasingly important features of the father's role. But as this brief overview of human evolution indicates, the importance of father's direct caretaking role has varied dramatically over human history. One form of investment should not be considered more natural or better than another. For instance, there is no reason to believe that American fathers in the 1950s, who were primarily breadwinners rather than direct caregivers, were any better or worse than fathers in the 1980s, who were active caregivers and not sole providers to the family.

The second point of this evolutionary overview is to identify some of the limitations of the data on Aka Pygmy fathers. The Aka are hunter-gatherers, and it is true that 95 percent of human history is characterized by this lifestyle. But as table 45 indicates there are dramatic differences between the Late Pleistocene hunter-gatherers and Holocene hunter-gatherers like the Aka Pygmies. The data show that both were very mobile, subsisted on wild foods, and lived in small groups. But large game hunted by men were central to the diet of the Late Pleistocene hunter-gatherers, whereas gathering by men and women and hunting of medium sized game (usually by men, but sometimes by women) were important for the Holocene hunter-gatherers. These differences in the sexual division of labor and male-female contributions to the diet patterned different male-female and father-child relations. But the Aka and a few other hunter-gatherers *are* the last people on earth to live in small mobile groups similar to the hunter-gatherer groups living at the time of human evolutionary adaptiveness. While not ideal, they are essentially the best human populations to work with to try and understand human nature. There is much to learn about fathering from the Aka, but one has to be cautious in using the Aka data to make universal statements about the nature of fathers' roles.

THE ORIGIN OF FATHERS' ROLES

The discussion above identified different forms of fathers' investment in children and examined how important these various forms of investment have been for the last 120,000 years. In this section we go back further into human history and consider the origins of the different forms of male parental investment in humans. As mentioned above, the reconstruction of fathers' roles in human evolution should be considered heuristic and tentative.

The origin of male involvement in humans is usually linked to increased brain capacity, bipedalism, and the birth of altricial infants (Benshoof and Thornhill 1979). A consequence of human bipedalism and the marked increase in human cranial capacity is that the human infant is delivered in a less developed stage than is found with other higher primates, such as chimpanzee or gorilla infants. Newborn nonhuman primate infants, for instance, can grasp onto their mothers, while human infants cannot. The altricial human infant requires greater paternal care. Lancaster (1983), however, points out that human males generally do very little caregiving during infancy, and that men in most cultures become involved during early childhood (three to five years of age). She hypothesizes that human male involvement evolved as a result of greater care and

157

investment needed during weaning. As young children are weaned they need more attention from someone other than mother, who is usually pregnant or has another infant. The young children need more supplemental feedings to ensure their health and survival. Lancaster suggests that the father's role as caregiver and provider evolved as a result of the child's needs at this age. Consistent with this hypothesis is the proposition by Mackey (1985) that father involvement is linked to the human male propensity to share hunted meat with wife and children. He points out that some male social carnivores (coyote, jackal, and hunting dog) provide both care and hunted meat to their offspring, whereas other male social carnivores who do not share their meat (lion and hyena) also do not provide any direct offspring care. "The level of paternal behavior does seem more consonant with that found in social carnivores which have their males sharing food with their young (69)."

The theories seem reasonable but are based upon few data. Altriciality associated with bipedalism is the most common factor cited for increased male parental investment in humans, but altriciality cannot be a prime mover as there are numerous animal species that have altricial young but also have males that provide no food or care to offspring. In order to test Lancaster's hypothesis about the origins of male parental care, the sixty societies in the Human Relations Area Files Probability Sample (Lagace 1979) were examined for data on the father's role in infancy and childhood. The cross-cultural study supported Lancaster's contention that cross-culturally fathers do very little with infants. Only thirty-one societies, for instance, had data on father holding during infancy. Of the thirty-one societies with such data, fathers never held the infant in five societies, occasionally held the infant in twenty-three societies, and held the infant on a regular basis in only three societies. Also, of fifty-two societies that listed the infants' primary caregivers only five mentioned the father as one of the primary caregivers. Lancaster's contention that fathers become more involved during early childhood was also not well supported. More societies had data on fathers' roles in early childhood (46), but in half of these societies fathers were not regular participants in childcare. Fathers that were described as regular participants in the care of three to five year olds were involved in the transmission of subsistence skills, not in the provision or direct care of the child. Fathers in many societies did not get involved with their children until they were adolescents. While there are numerous problems with using this cross-cultural sample (it is small and has few foraging populations, which better characterize the environment of evolutionary adaptiveness), it does question the notion that male parental investment is especially critical during early childhood. Mackey's theory also seems reasonable, but there is one feature of the group of social carnivores that share meat (the canids) that he does not mention—their basic groups consists of permanent or at least seasonal pair-bonds. Foxes, jackals, and coyotes live in permanent mated pairs. There seems to be immense tolerance between males and females in canid species that share meat (Rasa 1986).

Building upon the work of Smuts (1985) I would suggest that male parental investment in humans evolved out of increasing male-female reciprocity. Altriciality, bipedalism, and a movement toward decreased birth spacing (Lovejoy 1981) all played a part, but it was the nature of male-female relations that became a prime factor in the evolution of the father's role. The following overview of early human evolution examines the origin of the different forms of male parental investment.

The Australopithecines are the earliest members of the human family and lived four to one million years ago on the edge of the forests in East Africa. They were bipedal, three-and-one-half-to-five feet tall, weighed about eighty pounds, and had a cranial capacity of about 450 cubic centimeters. They lived in very small groups (maybe five to ten individuals), were primarily gatherers, relied some on scavenging for meat, and had a rudimentary stone toolkit. With the exception of the mother providing food to her young, sharing was minimal as everyone gathered for himself/herself. Since their brain capacity was not large (similar in size to modern great apes) infants were not altricial (Trevathan 1987). Australopithecine

infants were possibly able to cling to their mothers and feed themselves at an earlier age. Male parental care emerged primarily out
of social rather than economic relations with particular females.
Meat from hunting was not important as everyone collected for
himself/herself, but defense would have been important as the Australopithecines were small and had few tools to defend themselves.
But male parental investment emerged in a rather indirect fashion.
Marriage or long-term (several years) male-female relationships
probably did not exist at this time. A male probably had extended
social relations with a particular female (called "friendships" by
Smuts [1985]) and would stay close to the female, providing protection and grooming for her and possibly her infant in exchange for
future sex with the female. The male might have used the infant as
an "agonistic buffer" in dealing with other males in the group (Taub
1985). These males probably provided occasional food and direct
care to the infant, but paternity certainty (knowing that the infant
was his) was probably not a condition for giving the food or care.
His primary interest was the infant's mother. In order for male
parental investment in humans to emerge, males had to get close to
the infants on a regular basis. This happened as a consequence of
male-female social and sexual relations, not because of paternity
certainty or the need for male-female economic exchange. It was
an indirect form of investment in that the male would perform the
activity regardless of the infant's presence or absence, but the infant
did accrue some benefits—protection from predators and other environmental dangers, including aggressive conspecifics.

Our own genus, *Homo,* emerged around 1.5 million years ago
and represented the next major stage of human evolution. The
lifeways of *Homo erectus* are described, while those of *Homo
habalis* are omitted because of the limited fossil and archaeological
data on this early hominid. *Homo erectus* lived about 1.6 million
to .35 million years ago, first in Africa, and eventually in Asia and
Europe. *Homo erectus* was bipedal, about five to six feet tall,
weighed one hundred to one hundred and fifty pounds, and had a
cranial capacity of about 1,100 cubic centimeters (over twice the

size of the Australopithecines). They lived in larger groups than the Australopithecines (five to seven families), relied much more extensively on hunting large game, and used a variety of modified stone tools. Due to the increase in brain capacity, infants were born at an earlier stage of development when they could pass through the birth canal. Male parental investment now included providing for the young. Males provided the bulk of the calories in the family diet as hunting became increasingly important. Long-term male-female arrangements ("marriage") emerged as economic cooperation between men and women developed (men as hunters, women as gatherers). With this economic exchange between men and women and an increase in the economic investment by men, paternity certainty became increasingly important. Since stone tools were still rather basic, the father's role as cultural transmitter though increasing was still limited. But fathers were substantially more proximal to their children than before for husband, wife, and children were living and sleeping together. The father's proximity provided his children the opportunity for indirect cultural transmission (observation and experimentation) as well as protection from dangers in the social and natural environment. Direct care of infants by most fathers was probably infrequent, but they knew their children well since they slept with them and were around them much of the day. Since males provided a substantial percentage of calories to the diet, it is unlikely that they were involved in much direct care of infants (see chap. 7), but they were probably important transporters of four-to-five-year-old children. These were mobile hunter-gatherers and young children would have had difficulty keeping up with the group. Mothers were probably carrying infants. Transporting children may have been the most consistent form of fathers' direct care. Some fathers who were not especially good hunters or who had few relatives to help their wives probably compensated for these shortcomings by providing more direct care to infants and children than males who were good hunters and had large families (Strassmann 1981 and chap. 7). Fathers' indirect investment as protectors of their families diminished from the previous stage because they had better

tools to defend themselves, were larger in size than the Australopithecines, had greater intelligence, and lived in larger groups.

It is possible that the father's *role* or social fatherhood slowly
emerged in this period. Increasing intelligence, increasing reciprocity between husband and wife and other camp members, increasing
importance of cultural transmission, and the movement of these
populations out of tropical Africa into a diversity of temperate environments in Eurasia made them more adaptive to intraspecies variability (roles adapted to a variety of environments).

Our own species, *Homo sapiens,* emerged around 120,000 years
ago in Africa. This final stage of human evolution to be considered
occurred in the Late Pleistocene era and has already been described
in the discussion of different forms of paternal investment. Only a
few additional comments are necessary. The Neanderthals and other
early *Homo sapiens* lived about 120,000–40,000 years ago in
Europe, Asia, and Africa. They were about the same size as contemporary humans and had about the same brain capacity. The
Neanderthals were shorter and more robust than other early *Homo
sapiens*. Early *Homo sapiens* had extensive and diverse stone tools
in comparison to *Homo erectus*. Large game hunting appears to
have been even more important than with *Homo erectus*. The Neanderthals were the first humans to systematically bury their dead,
possibly with grave goods, the earliest evidence of belief in an
afterlife and religion. The features of male investment described at
the *Homo erectus* stage became more pronounced at the *Homo
sapiens* stage. With a greater reliance on large game, providing
became an even more important feature of male parental investment. As subsistence and cultural life became more complex, the
father's role as direct cultural transmitter became vital to the fitness
and survival of his children. The father's role in early *Homo sapiens*
society is essentially the same as that described for fathers in the
Late Pleistocene era.

Regular direct care of infants and the importance of inheritance
evolved relatively late in human history. Direct care seems to be
especially common among hunter-gatherers who emphasize gather-

ing, and inheritance emerges with horticulture and collecting but becomes especially important with intensive farming (table 46).

This is a very brief and speculative description of the origins of different forms of male parental investment in humans. Direct caregiving was not a substantial aspect of the father's investment until the emergence of the Holocene hunter-gatherers. Carrying of children three to four years of age while moving from camp to camp was probably an early and important form of direct care provided by *Homo erectus* and *Homo sapiens* fathers. Proximity provided protection to the infant and was the earliest form of male parental investment in humans. The importance of proximity increased at the last two stages described because males were more likely to be the biological fathers of the children they were caring for and fathers usually slept with their families and were available while in camp. Cultural transmission became increasingly important as culture complexity increased. The kin network provided by father was probably important throughout these periods of human evolution.

This brief overview of the origin and development of different forms of male parental investment in humans emphasizes the following points. First, the origin and nature of male parental investment in humans often emerge as a result of male-female or husband-wife relationships. From Australopithecines to *Homo sapiens*, the nature of male-female or husband-wife social, economic, and sexual relations reflects the nature of the father-child relationship. Second, the earliest substantial form of male (though not necessarily the

TABLE 46.   The Evolution of Various Forms of Direct Male Parental Investment in Humans

Form of Male Parental Investment	Emergence (years ago)
Proximity (protection)	4 million
Economic contributor	1.6 million
Proximity maintenance (monitor, cult. trans.)	1.6 million
Cultural transmission (direct)	120 thousand
Direct caretaking	12 thousand
Inheritance	5 thousand

natural father) investment among humans was probably an indirect form of protection and emerged from male-female social relationships rather than male-female economic relationships. Only with the emergence of large game hunting and the birth of altricial infants does the father's role as economic provider become important.

THE DEFICIT MODEL

The introduction of the book stated that an underlying "deficit" model existed in current cross-cultural child development studies. Fathers are consistently *not* involved in childcare so their role in child development is seldom if ever discussed. Fathers are often forgotten or their role is minimized. This chapter has pointed out that fathers can contribute to their children in a number of ways, and that a father's contribution may not be direct. Psychologists and anthropologists tend to emphasize involvement as an important aspect of the father's role, in large part, because of the economic, social, and emotional demands of our own neolocal urban life. Father involvement is important today and it is an important feature of the Aka father's role, but this does not mean it is universal or natural for fathers to be active caregivers. The Aka data clearly suggest men are capable of providing care to very young infants.

One feature of the father's role is emerging from anthropological studies: Fetal, infant, and child morbidity and mortality increase if one does not have a father. Fathers are important regardless of their absence-presence or aloofness-intimacy. Spontaneous abortion increases when pregnancy is illegitimate, when a father loses his job, when there are disharmonious marital relations, or when a father dies (Chisholm 1984). Hill and Kaplan (1988) report that Ache child mortality increases significantly if the father dies or leaves the family. Pennington and Harpending (1988) describe a similar pattern among the !Kung San. Bugos and McCarthy (1984) report that the most common reasons for infanticide among the Ayoreo of South America were desertion of the mother by the father and the mother's fear that her husband would desert her. I have already reported the risk of mortality for Aka infants if no father is identified. Fathers in these different cultures contribute to their children in vastly different ways. For instance, Ache men are hunters and provide 85 percent of the calories to the diet, !Kung men are hunters but provide only 30 percent of the calories to the family diet. Ayoreo men are simple farmers and provide a small percentage of the calories to the diet, and Aka men provide about 50 percent of the calories to the diet. Regardless of the father's role as provider, fathers are still important in other ways that are essential to the child's survival and health.

The father's role is a complex issue, and there are a number of ecological, social, demographic, and other factors that can influence its expression in a particular culture. Due to this complexity, it will often be difficult to determine specifically how fathers influence the physical, social, and emotional development of children.

CHAPTER 9

Conclusions and Implications

This book has given a detailed account of the Aka Pygmy father-infant relationship. Emphasis has been placed on the level and context of father involvement, and style of father-infant interactions (as compared to mother and others). It is the first extensive study of the father-infant relationship in a non-Western population at the band or tribal level. Although primarily descriptive and based on a limited data set (few individuals, few observations, over a short six-month period) some data relative to major theoretical issues on fathering were also presented. This final chapter summarizes the major ethnographic and theoretical results of the Aka father-infant study and considers possible implications of the Aka father-infant study for Euroamerican fathers.

The significant ethnographic features of the father-infant relationship are summarized below:

1. Aka fathers do more infant caregiving than fathers in any other known society. A number of ecological, social, ideological, and demographic factors contributed to the high level of father involvement, but three factors were identified as being especially influential: the requirements of the net hunt, the husband-wife relationship, and father-infant attachment. Other factors that promoted or were consistent with greater father involvement included: lack of warfare and violence, especially against women and children; an egalitarian ideology; high fertility rates; and, near equal contribution to the diet by males and females.

167

2. Unlike U.S. fathers, Aka fathers are not the vigorous, rough-and-tumble playmates of their infants. The lack of physical play among Aka fathers may be a consequence of Aka fathers being more familiar with their infants, knowing infant caregiving practices well, and valuing infant caregiving (infant caretaking is not seen as feminine). Aka culture generally does not promote physical and aggressive play, while in the United States these behaviors are encouraged (e.g., through competitive sports).

3. The Aka father's role can be characterized by its intimate, affectionate, helping-out nature, rather than by its playfulness. Aka fathers spend 47 percent of their day holding or within an arm's reach of their infants, and while holding the infant, father is more likely than mother to hug and kiss the infant. The father's caregiving often takes place while the mother is carrying a heavy load, collecting firewood, or preparing a meal. Aka conceptions of good and bad fathers also reiterate these roles—a good father should show love (affection) for his children, stay near them, and assist mother with caregiving when her workload is heavy. A bad father abandons his children and does not share food with them. When adolescents were asked who played more with them when they were children, just as many said father as said mother.

4. Father-infant caregiving varies with social and subsistence setting. Fathers are most likely to hold and be within proximity of their infants while in camp talking with other males. They are least likely to hold their infants outside of camp while engaged in economic activity.

5. Greater availability is not related to greater father caregiving. Fathers in the village do just as much caregiving as fathers in the forest even though they are much less available during the day.

6. Time allocation data indicate that fathers who do considerable direct caregiving as well as those who do little caretaking spend similar amounts of time in subsistence and manufacturing activities, but fathers who do less caretaking spend more time visiting and talking with other males. Aka fathers less involved in direct caretaking seem to spend more time in "status maintenance."

7. Aka fathers with more kin and material resources provided less direct care of infants than fathers with fewer kin and material resources. Fathers with fewer kin were also more likely to have had stepfathers at a young age. Two explanations were offered for the intracultural variability in father involvement: (1) a trade-off explanation—women would select males without kin and material resources if they knew the men would be willing to help with infant and child care, and (2) a task assignment explanation—men with stepfathers were given more "feminine" tasks.

The Aka ethnographic data have implications for psychological, sociological, and anthropological theory. The various theoretical implications are summarized below:

1. The Aka do not fit Lamb's (1981) attachment theory hypothesis. Vigorous play by fathers may not be the only means by which infants: (1) become attached to their fathers, and (2) initially learn social competence. Aka infants apparently become attached to their fathers as a consequence of fathers' greater (than American fathers') emotional and physical involvement. The Aka father's caregiving style is distinct from that of the mother and may contribute to early acquisition of social competence, but the caregiving style of "other" caregivers is also distinct from that of the mother and father, so others may also contribute to the initial social competence of the infant.
2. The Aka do not fit Parsons and Bales's (1955) male-instrumental: female-expressive role dichotomy theory. Aka fathers are nurturing and affectionate with their children and are not family disciplinarians fostering social competence. Mothers are usually the disciplinarians and are regular providers to the family diet.
3. The Aka do not fit LaRossa and LaRossa's (1981) intrinsic-extrinsic and role-embracement, role-distance, mother-father parenting dichotomies found in American families. Aka fathers intrinsically value parenting and embrace their parenting role.
4. The Aka do fit the Whiting and Whiting (1975) model, which

predicts that fathers will provide more childcare in societies where husband-wife relations are intimate (rather than aloof) and material goods cannot be accumulated. Aka have few material goods that can be accumulated due to their mobile lifestyle, and Aka husband and wife spend considerable time together in cooperative subsistence activities.

This study also has implications for field methodologies used by cross-cultural child development researchers. Previous researchers made most, if not all, of their observations in the camp setting where it is easier to record observations and have access to focal subjects. For instance, the research of Melvin Konner (1977) and Patricia Draper (1976) among the !Kung San and the infant and child development work of Winn, Morelli, and Tronick (1990) among the Efe in the Ituri are all of exceptional quality, but the results of their work are limited because all of their behavioral observations were made in camp settings. When one reads that !Kung infants nurse four times an hour or that Efe infants have an average transfer rate (number of people who hold infant in given time period) of five per hour, it is essential to understand that these data apply to camp settings only. The results of Mackey's (1985) extensive cross-cultural study of the father-child bond are even more limiting: all observations of men with children were conducted in public places (e.g., playgrounds). The Aka data demonstrate the dramatic differences in fathers' behavior in a variety of social and subsistence contexts.

This was also the first cross-cultural child development study to conduct observations in the early evening and use father focal observations. The study demonstrated the importance of early evening hour observations as Aka fathers provided substantial care after sundown. During daylight hours, Aka fathers held their infants about 9 percent of the time, but between the hours of 6:30 P.M. and 9:00 P.M. fathers held their infants about 20 percent of the time. Caregiving patterns change in the evening as camp activities change. The evening is particularly noted for its collective singing, dancing, and ritual life. The father focal observations were also very useful for understanding the nature of the father's role. Father focal observations made it possible to examine intracultural variability in father involvement—to determine what fathers were doing if they were not engaged in infant care. Future child development studies should also attempt systematic observations throughout the night. Infants in all cultures wake often during the night, and it is my impression that fathers are often involved in infants' care during this time. Among the Aka, it was not uncommon to wake up in the middle of the night and hear a father singing softly to his fussing infant.

Implications for Contemporary American Fathers and Mothers

The Aka study may have some implications for contemporary American parents. The Aka and American social contexts are dramatically different, and it is impossible to transplant aspects of Aka culture into American culture, but I do believe that parents in the United States can learn from Aka parents and children.

First, the Aka demonstrate that there are cultural systems where men can be active, intimate and nurturing caregivers. American subcultures and counterculture movements have encouraged men to be active caregivers, but they had to have strong convictions to persist in mainstream U.S. culture. Men and women who are trying to promote active care by men have a difficult time because they have no salient and intimate models to draw upon. The Aka extend our understanding of human potential.

Second, the Aka data may have implications for understanding the nature and consequences of "quality" versus "quantity" time. Western psychological research indicates that children can be securely attached to parents who spend little time with them (who do not spend "quantity time" because they work all day), if the parents spend "quality" time with their children once they get home. Secure parent-child attachment is important because it presumably predicts emotional and social well-being later in life. Quality time means the

171

parent gives his or her undivided attention to the child somewhat like the attention one gives to a lover. American quality time often becomes playtime, and it is clear that parents are attempting to demonstrate their love and concern for the child in quality time. It is reasonable to assume that parent-child psychological attachment does take place. But it is important to remember that psychologists measure attachment in a twenty-one minute "strange situation" test. It has been demonstrated that this psychological test only measures current parent-child relations and does not predict emotional and psychological well-being later in life (Lamb et al. 1984).

The Aka data point to the importance of quantity time rather than quality time. Aka fathers do provide some quality time, but most (about 75 percent) of their time with infants is spent in basic caregiving (holding, watching, feeding). The Aka father-child relationship is intimate not because of quality time but because the father knows his child exceptionally well through regular interaction. Aka fathers do not often play with their infants because they can communicate their love and concern in other ways. They know subtle means of interacting with their children. They sleep with their infants and have physical contact throughout the day. The Aka data suggest that intimate parent-child relations contribute to emotional security. I would suggest that the intimate parent-child relations contribute substantially to the development of autonomy and self-assuredness. Aka children develop these characteristics at a very early age (five to six years old), while it may take a lifetime for many Americans. It is impossible for American parents today to spend as much time with their children as Aka parents do, but the Aka data do suggest that whenever possible it is important for American parents to hold or be near their children. This may mean sleeping with young children, taking children to adult activities, holding infants more often rather than letting them sit in infant carrying devices, or allowing children to play around grown-ups engaged in adult activities.

Third, the Aka study, as well as studies of social carnivores and nonhuman primates, indicates that the male-female/husband-wife relationship is an important predictor of male-infant/father-infant relations. Aka husband and wife are together much of the day and they have multistranded reciprocity, that is, they help each other in a diversity of domains—subsistence, food preparation, and child-care. Aka husband and wife do not hug, kiss, and show other forms of physical affection common to American male-female relations, but Aka husband and wife engage in all kinds of playful activities and appear to enjoy each other's company as well as cooperating together in subsistence and other activities. This suggests that before American father-child relations improve or change, husband-wife relations are probably going to have to change.

Fourth, the Aka study indicates that stepparenting and single parenting are common because of divorce and adult mortality. These patterns are not unique to the Aka; they are common features of childcare cross-culturally (Hewlett 1990). Due to increasing divorce rates in the United States, the American family is often said to be decaying, declining, threatened, or endangered. One gets the impression from the popular and professional literature that a life-long husband-wife pair-bond is natural and universal, and that step-parenting is unusual and abnormal. Margaret Mead pointed out some time ago that divorce in American society is perceived as a sign of personal and social failure. American perceptions about divorce and stepparents have not changed much. The Aka data clearly point out that the breakdown or decay of the family is not a unique feature of contemporary industrialized societies and that stepparenting is part of our human heritage. The American family is not endangered; it is simply changing. While stepparenting is common cross-culturally, very little is known about stepparent-step-child relations. Future child development studies should consider this topic.

Finally, the contemporary Western sociological and psychological literature is concerned with the consequences of increased paternal involvement. As more American mothers go to work and more fathers become involved with caregiving, Americans want to know the consequences of greater father involvement. The positive consequences of greater paternal involvement are emphasized. Chodorow (1973), for instance, states that:

> boys need to grow up around men who take a major role in child care, and girls around women who, in addition to their child-care responsibilities, have a valued role and recognized spheres of legitimate control. These arrangements could help to ensure that children of both sexes develop a sufficiently individuate and strong sense of self, as well as a positively valued and secure gender identity, that does not bog down wither in ego-boundary confusion, low self-esteem and overwhelming relatedness to others, or in compulsive denial of any connection to others or dependence upon them. (66)

Chodorow predicts that in an ideal society where fathers are intimate identity figures for their sons (always available as mothers are to daughters), and fathers are active participants in infant care, that males would be less dominating over women and less likely to reject those things symbolizing femininity. The Aka are probably the only society known today where these two conditions are met. Due to the high availability and active caregiving of their fathers, Aka males may not be as rejecting of feminine things, such as infant care, gathering, and food preparation. Infant care in most societies is perceived as symbolizing femininity, in part, because of the infant's dependency on its mother for frequent nursing; yet in many societies males perceive infant care as threatening to their masculinity. Kaplan (1988), for instance, says that if an Ache man carried a three-month-old infant in a sling he would be called a homosexual by the other Ache men. Aka fathers do not perceive or act as though infant care has a bearing upon their masculinity, and they demonstrate intrinsic satisfaction while caregiving. A problem with the Chodorow hypothesis is that other consequences predicted from greater paternal involvement and availability (less competitiveness and more solidarity and commitment to the group) are found among the Aka, but also found among the !Kung and other foraging populations where fathers are not as involved in childcare. This suggests that the egalitarian ideologies, lack of violence against women, and other features of foraging societies are just as influential as father involvement in predicting greater sexual equality.

References Cited

Ainsworth, M. D. S.
1967 *Infancy in Uganda: Infant Care and the Growth of Love.* Baltimore: Johns Hopkins Press.
1977 Attachment Theory and Its Utility in Cross-Cultural Research. In *Culture and Infancy: Variations in the Human Experience*, ed. P. H. Leiderman et al. New York: Academic Press.

Altman, J.
1974 Observational Study of Behaviour. *Behaviour* 49:227–67.
1980 *Baboon Mothers and Infants.* Cambridge, Mass.: Harvard University Press.

Anderson, R. E.
1968 Where's Dad? Paternal Deprivation and Delinquency. *Archives of General Psychiatry* 18:641–49.

Arco, C. M. B.
1983 Pacing of Playful Stimulation to Young Infants: Similarities and Differences in Maternal and Paternal Communication. *Infant Behavior and Development* 6:223–28.

Babchuk, W. A., R. B. Hames, and R. A. Thompson
1985 Sex Differences in the Recognition of Infant Facial Expressions of Emotion: The Primary Caretaker Hypothesis. *Ethology and Sociobiology* 6:89–101.

Bacon, M. K., I. L. Child, and H. Barry
1963 A Cross-Cultural Study of Correlates of Crime. *Journal of Abnormal and Social Psychology* 66:291–300.

References Cited

Bahuchet, S.
1975 Rapport sur Une Mission Effectuee en Saison Seche en Lobaye (Republique Centrafricaine). *Journal d'Agric. Tropicale et de Botanique* 23:177–97.
1985 *Les Pygmees Aka et la Foret Centrafricaine.* Paris: Selaf.
1987 Historical Perspectives on the Aka and Baka Pygmies in the Western Congo Basin. Paper presented at the American Anthropological Association Meetings, Chicago, Illinois.
1988 Food Supply and Uncertainty Among Aka Pygmies (Lobaye, Central African Republic). In *Coping with Uncertainty in Food Supply,* ed. I. de Garine and G. A. Harrison. Oxford: Oxford University Press.
Bahuchet, S., and H. Guillaume
1982 Aka-Farmer Relations in the Northwest Congo Basin. In *Politics and History in Band Societies,* ed. E. Leacock and R. B. Lee. Cambridge: Cambridge University Press.
Bailey, R. C.
1985 The Socioecology of Efe Pygmy Men in the Ituri Forest, Zaire. Ph.D. diss. Harvard University.
1989 The Demography of the Efe and Lese of the Ituri Forest, Zaire. Paper presented at the American Anthropological Association Meetings, Washington, D.C.
Bailey, R. C., and N. R. Peacock
1988 Efe Pygmies of Northeast Zaire: Subsistence Strategies in the Ituri Forest. In *Coping with Uncertainty in Food Supply,* ed. I. de Garine and G. A. Harrison. Oxford: Oxford University Press.
Bailey, R. C., G. Head, M. Jenike, B. Owen, R. Rechtman, and E. Zechenter
1989 Hunting and Gathering in Tropical Rain Forest: Is It Possible? *American Anthropologist* 91:59–82.
Bateman, A. J.
1948 Intra-Sexual Selection in Drosophila. *Heredity* 2:349–68.
Barry, H., III, and L. M. Paxson
1971 Infancy and Early Childhood: Cross-Cultural Codes 2. *Ethology* 10:466–508.

Bayle des Hermes, R. de
1973   *Recherches Prehistoriques en Republique Centrafricaine*. Paris: Editions Labethno.

Belsky, J.
1980   A Family Analysis of Parental Influence on Infant Exploratory Competence. In *The Father-Infant Relationship*, ed. F. A. Pedersen. New York: Praeger.

Benshoof, L., and R. Thornhill
1979   The Evolution of Monogamy and Concealed Ovulation in Humans. *Social and Biological Structures* 2:95–106.

Betzig, L., A. Harrigan, and P. Turke
1990   Childcare on Ifaluk. *Zeitscrift fur Ethnologie* 114 (in press).

Binford, L. R.
1968   Post-Pleistocene Adaptations. In *New Perspectives in Archaeology*, ed. S. R. Binford and L. R. Binford. Chicago: Aldine.

Birdsell, J. B.
1973   A Basic Demographic Unit. *Current Anthropology* 14:337–50.

Block, J., A. van der Lippe, and J. H. Block
1973   Sex role and Socialization: Some Personality Concomitants and Environmental Antecedents. *Journal of Consulting and Clinical Psychology* 41:321–41.

Borgerhoff Mulder, M., and T. Caro
1985   The Use of Quantitative Observational Techniques in Anthropology. *Current Anthropology* 26:325–35.

Borgerhoff Mulder, M., and M. Milton
1985   Factors Affecting Infant Care in the Kipsigis. *Journal of Anthropological Research* 41:231–62.

Bowlby, J.
1969   *Attachment and Loss*. Vol. 1: *Attachment*. New York: Basic Books.

Bronfenbrenner, U.
1961   Some Familial Antecedents of Responsibility and Leadership in Adolescents. In *Leadership and Interpersonal Behavior*, ed. L. Petrullo and B. M. Bass. New York: Holt, Rinehart and Winston.
1979   *The Ecology of Human Development*. Cambridge, Mass.: Harvard University Press.

References Cited

Brown, J. K.
1970 A Note on the Division of Labor by Sex. *American Anthropologist* 72:1073–78.

Bugos, P. E., and L. McCarthy
1984 Ayoreo Infanticide: A Case Study. In *Infanticide: Comparative and Evolutionary Perspectives*, ed. G Hausfater and S. Blaffer Hrdy. Hawthorne, N. Y.: Aldine.

Burbank, V., and J. Chisholm
1989 Gender Differences in Parental Expectations. Paper presented at the American Anthropological Association Meetings, Washington, D.C.

Burton, M., L. A. Brudner, and D. R. White
1977 A Model for the Sexual Division of Labor. *American Ethnologist* 4:227–52.

Carneiro, R. L.
1970 A Theory of the Origin of State. *Science* 169:733–38.

Cavalli-Sforza, L. L. ed.
1986 *African Pygmies*. New York: Academic Press.

Cavalli-Sforza, L. L., and M. W. Feldman
1981 *Cultural Transmission and Evolution: A Quantitative Approach*. Princeton, N. J.: Princeton University Press.

Chagnon, N. A.
1968 *Yanomamö: The Fierce People*. 1st ed. New York: Holt, Rinehart and Winston.

1979 Is Reproductive Success Equal in Egalitarian Societies? In *Evolutionary Biology and Human Social Behavior: An Anthropological Perspective*, ed. Napoleon A. Chagnon and William Irons. North Scituate, Mass.: Duxbury Press.

1982 Sociodemographic Attributes of Nepotism in Tribal Populations: Man the Rule Breaker. In *Current Problems in Sociobiology*, ed. Brian Bertram et al. Cambridge: Cambridge University Press.

1988 Yanomamö Kinship Classification and Genealogical Knowledge by Sex: Male Manipulation of Female Classification for Reproductive Advantage. In *Human Reproductive Behaviour*, ed. L. Betzig, M. Borgerhoff Mulder, and P. Turke. Cambridge: Cambridge University Press.

Chisholm, J.
  1983   *Navajo Infancy: An Ethological Study of Child Development.*
         Hawthorne, N.Y.: Aldine.
  1984   A Biosocial View of Prenatal Influences. Paper presented at the
         American Anthropological Association Meetings, Denver,
         Colorado.
Chodorow, N.
  1973   Family Structure and Feminine Personality. In *Woman, Culture
         and Society,* ed. M. Z. Rosaldo and Louise Lamphere. Stanford,
         Calif.: Stanford University Press.
Clarke-Stewart, K. A.
  1978   And Daddy Makes Three: The Father's Impact on Mother and
         Young Child. *Child Development* 49:466–78.
  1980   The Father's Contribution to Children's Cognitive and Social
         Development in Early Childhood. In *The Father-Infant Rela-
         tionship,* ed. F. A. Pedersen. New York: Praeger.
Cole, M., and J. S. Bruner
  1974   Cultural Differences and Inferences about Psychological Pro-
         cesses. In *Culture and Cognition,* ed. J. W. Berry and P. R.
         Dasen. London: Methuen.
Coleman, A. D.
  1981   *Earth Father/Sky Father: The Changing Concept of Fathering.*
         Englewood Cliffs, N.J.: Prentice-Hall.
Cordes, L., and B. S. Hewlett
  1990   Health and Nutrition of Aka Pygmies. Paper presented at the
         International Conference on Hunting and Gathering Societies,
         Fairbanks, Alaska.
Crawley, S. B., and K. B. Sherrod
  1984   Parent-Infant Play During the First Year of Life. *Infant Behavior
         and Development* 7:65–75.
Darwin, C.
  1871   *The Descent of Man, and Selection in Relation to Sex.* New
         York: Appleton.
David, N.
  1980   Early Bantu Expansion in the Context of Central African Prehis-
         tory: 4000–1 B.C. In *L'Espansion Bantoue,* vol. 2., ed. L.
         Bouxiaux. Paris: Selaf.

References Cited

Denham, W.
1974   Population Structure, Infant Transport, and Infanticide Among Modern and Pleistocene Hunter-Gatherers. *Journal of Anthropological Research* 30(3):191–98.

Deuss, J.
1968   *Conditions Climatiques du Centre de Recherche Agronomiques de Boukoko (R.C.A.): 27 Ans d'Observations Meteorologiques.* Paris: Cafe Cacao.

Dongier, R.
1953   Rapport d'Inspection de la Region Lobaye. No. 24/AA 1. Archives de la Prefecture de la Lobaye *(Mbaiki, R.C.A.).*

Draper, P.
1976   Social and Economic Constraints on Child Life among the !Kung. In *Kalahari Hunter-Gatherers*, ed. R. B. Lee and I. DeVore. Cambridge, Mass.: Harvard University Press.

Draper, P., and H. Harpending
1982   Father Absence and Reproductive Strategy: An Evolutionary Perspective. *Journal of Anthropological Research* 38:255–73.

Dunn, F.
1968   Epidemiological Factors: Health and Disease in Hunter-Gatherers. In *Man the Hunter*, ed. R. B. Lee and I. DeVore. Chicago: Aldine.

Durkheim, E.
1933   *The Division of Labor in Society.* Trans. by George Simpson. New York: MacMillan.

Early, J., and J. Peters
1990   *Population Dynamics of the Macajai Yanomamö.* New York: Academic Press.

Ember, C.
1973   Feminine Task Assignment and the Social Behavior of Boys. *Ethos* 1:424–39.

Emlen, S. T., and L. W. Oring
1977   Ecology, Sexual Selection, and the Evolution of Mating Systems. *Science* 197:215–23.

Erasmus, C.J.
1955   Work Patterns in a Mayo Village. *American Anthropologist* 57(2):322–33.

Field, T.
1978   Interaction Behaviors of Primary Versus Secondary Caretaker Fathers. *Developmental Psychology* 14:183–84.

Fish, K. D., and H. B. Biller
1973   Perceived Childhood Paternal Relationships and College Females' Personal Adjustment. *Adolescence* 8:415–20.

Foley, R.
1986   Spot the Difference: Evolutionary Perspectives on Hominids, Humans and Hunter-Gatherers. Paper presented at the International Conference on Hunting and Gathering Societies, London, England.

Fortes, M.
1938   Social and Psychological Aspects of Education in Taleland. *Africa* 11(3):14–90.

1958   Introduction. In *The Development Cycle in Domestic Groups*, ed. Jack Goody. Cambridge: Cambridge University Press.

Freedman, D. G.
1974   *Human Infancy: An evolutionary approach*. New York: John Wiley and Sons.

Freud, S.
1938   *An Outline of Psychoanalysis*. London: Hogarth.

Giglioli, E. H.
1880   Ulteriori Notizie Intorno ai Negriti. *Bollettino di Scienze Naturali della Societa Adriatica* V:404–11.

Goody, J.
1959   The Mother's Brother and the Sister's Son in West Africa. *Journal of the Royal Anthropological Institute* 89:61–88.

1973   Bridewealth and Dowry in Africa and Eurasia. In *Bridewealth and Dowry*, ed. J. R. Goody and S. J. Tambiah. Cambridge: Cambridge University Press.

Greenberg, J.H.
1963   *The Languages of Africa*. The Hague: Mouton.

Hames, R. B.
1978   A Behavioral Account of the Division of Labor Among the Ye'kwana. Ph.D. Diss. University of California, Santa Barbara.

1979   Relatedness and Interaction Among the Ye'kwana: A Preliminary Analysis. In *Evolutionary Biology and Human Social Be-*

havior: An Anthropological Perspective, ed. Napoleon A. Chagnon and William Irons. North Scituate, Mass.: Duxbury Press.

1988   The Allocation of Parental Care Among the Ye'kwana. In *Human Reproductive Behaviour*, ed. L. Betzig, M. Borgerhoff Mulder, and P. Turke. Cambridge: Cambridge University Press.

Hamilton, A.
1981   *Nature and Nurture: Aboriginal Child-Rearing in North-Central Arnhem land.* Canberra: Australian Institute of Aboriginal Studies.

Harlow, H. F.
1961   The Development of Affectional Patterns in Infant Monkeys. In *Determinants of Infant Behavior,* vol. 1, ed. B. M. Foss. London: Methuen.

Harpending, H.
1976   Regional Variation in !Kung Populations. In *Kalahari Hunter-Gatherers,* ed. R. B. Lee and I. DeVore. Cambridge, Mass.: Harvard University Press.

Hart, J.
1977   From Subsistence to Market: A Case Study of the Mbuti Net Hunters. *Human Ecology* 6:325–53.

Hart, T. B., and J. A. Hart
1986   The Ecological Basis of Hunter-Gatherer Subsistence in African Rain Forests: The Mbuti of Eastern Zaire. *Human Ecology* 14(1):29–55.

Hartung, J.
1985   Matrilineal Inheritance: New Theory and Analysis. *Behavioral and Brain Sciences* 8:661–68.

Hewlett, B. S.
1977   Notes on the Aka and Mbuti Pygmies of Central Africa. M.A. Thesis. California State University, Chico.

1987   Intimate Fathers: Paternal Patterns of Holding Among Aka Pygmies. In *Father's Role in Cross-Cultural Perspective*, ed. Michael E. Lamb. New York: Erlbaum.

1988a   Sexual Selection and Paternal Investment Among Aka Pygmies. In *Human Reproductive Behaviour*, ed. L. Betzig, M. Borgerhoff Mulder, P. Turke. Cambridge: Cambridge University Press.

1988b Dad and Cad Strategies: Father's Role in Human Evolution. Paper presentated at Evolution and Human Behavior Program, University of Michigan, Ann Arbor, Michigan.

1989a Multiple Caretaking Among African Pygmies. *American Anthropologist* 91:186–91.

1989b Husband-Wife Reciprocity and the Aka Father-Infant Relationship. Paper presented at the American Anthropological Association Meetings, Washington, D.C.

1990 Demography and Childcare of Hunter-Gatherers and Horticulturalists. Paper delivered at the Society for Cross-Cultural Research. Ontario, California.

Hewlett, B. S., and L. L. Cavalli-Sforza.

1986 Cultural Transmission among Aka Pygmies. *American Anthropologist* 88:15–32.

Hewlett, B. S., J. M. H. van de Koppel, and L. L. Cavalli-Sforza

1982 Exploration Ranges of Aka Pygmies of the Central African Republic. *Man,* n.s. 17:418–30.

1986 Exploration and Mating Range of Aka Pygmies of the Central African Republic. In *African Pygmies,* ed. L. L. Cavalli-Sforza. New York: Academic Press.

Hewlett, B. S., J. M. H. van de Koppel, and M. van de Koppel

1986 Causes of Death among Aka Pygmies of the Central African Republic. In *African Pygmies*, ed. L. L. Cavalli-Sforza. New York: Academic Press.

Hill, K. and H. Kaplan

1988 Tradeoffs in Male and Female Reproductive Strategies among the Ache. In *Human Reproductive Behaviour*, ed. L. Betzig, M. Borgerhoff Mulder, and P. Turke. Cambridge: Cambridge University Press.

Hill, K., H. Kaplan, K. Hawkes, and A. M. Hurtado

1985 Men's Time Allocation to Subsistence Work among the Ache of Eastern Paraguay. *Human Ecology* 13:29–47.

Hoffman, M. L.

1981 The Role of the Father in Moral Internalization. In *The Role of the Father in Child Development*. 2d. ed. Ed. Michael E. Lamb. New York: John Wiley and Sons.

References Cited

Howell, N.
  1979 *Demography of the Dobe !Kung.* New York: Academic Press.
Hurtado, A. M.
  1985 Women's Subsistence Strategies among Ache Hunter-Gatherers of Eastern Paraguay. Ph.D. diss. University of Utah.
Johnson, A.
  1975 Time Allocation in a Machiguenga Community. *Ethnology* 14:301–10.
Kagan, J., and J. Lempkin
  1960 The Child's Differential Perception of Parental Attitudes. *Journal of Abnormal and Social Psychology* 61:440–47.
Kaplan, H.
  1988 Personal communication.
Katz, M. M., and M. J. Konner
  1981 The Role of Father: An Anthropological Perspective. In *The Role of the Father in Child Development.* 2d. ed. Ed. Michael E. Lamb. New York: John Wiley and Sons.
Kisliuk, M.
  1990 Rethinking Egalitarianism: Women's Dances among the Biaka Pygmies. Paper presented at the International Conference on Hunting and Gathering Societies, Fairbanks, Alaska.
Kleiman, D. G., and J. R. Malcolm
  1981 The Evolution of Male Parental Investment in Mammals. In *Parental Care in Mammals*, ed. D. J. Gubernick and P. H. Klopfer. New York: Plenum.
Konner, M. J.
  1976 Maternal Care, Infant Behavior and Development among the !Kung. In *Kalahari Hunter-Gatherers*, ed. R. B. Lee and I. DeVore. Cambridge, Mass.: Harvard University Press.
  1977 Infancy Among the Kalahari Desert San. In *Culture and Infancy: Variations in the Human Experience*, ed. P. H. Leiderman et al. New York: Academic Press.
Lagace, R. O.
  1979 The HRAF Probability Sample: Retrospect and Prospect. *Behavior Science Research* 14:211–29.

Lamb, M. E.
1976   *The Role of the Father in Child Development*. New York: John Wiley and Sons.
1977a The Development of Mother-Infant and Father-Infant Attachments in the Second Year of Life. *Developmental Psychology* 13:637–48.
1977b Father-Infant and Mother-Infant Interaction in the First Year of Life. *Child Development* 48:167–81.
1981   *The Role of the Father in Child Development*. 2d ed. New York: John Wiley and Sons.
1985   Observational Studies of Father-Child Relationships in Humans. In *Primate Paternalism*, ed. David Milton Taub. New York: Van Nostrand Reinhold.
Lamb, M. E., A. M. Frodi, M. Frodi, and C. P. Hwang
1982   Characteristics of Maternal and Paternal Behavior in Traditional and Non-Traditional Swedish Families. *International Journal of Behavior Development* 5:131–51.
Lamb, M. E., M. Frodi, C. P. Hwang, A. M. Frodi
1983   Effects of Paternal Involvement on Infant Preferences for Mothers and Fathers. *Child Development* 54:450–58.
Lamb, M. E., J. H. Pleck, E. L. Charnov, and J. A. LeVine
1987   A Biosocial Perspective on Paternal Behavior and Involvement. In *Parenting Across the Lifespan*, ed. J. B. Lancaster, J. Altmann, A. Rossi, L. R. Sherrod. Hawthorne, N.Y.: Aldine.
Lamb, M. E., R. A. Thompson, W. P. Gardner, E. L. Charnov, and D. Estes
1984   Security of Infantile Attachment as Assessed in the "Strange Situation": Its Study and Biological Interpretation. *The Behavioral and Brain Sciences* 7:127–71.
Lancaster, J. C.
1983   Evolutionary Perspectives on Sex Differences in the Higher Primates. In *Gender and the Life Course*, ed. Alice S. Rossi. Hawthorne, N.Y.: Aldine.
Lancaster, J. B., and C. S. Lancaster
1987   The Watershed: Change in Parental-Investment and Family For-

mation Strategies in the Course of Human Evolution. In *Parenting Across the Lifespan*, ed. J. B. Lancaster, J. Altmann, A. S. Rossi and L. R. Sherrod. Hawthorne, N.Y.: Aldine.

LaRossa, R., and M. M. LaRossa
  1981 *Transition to Parenthood: How Infants Change Families*. Beverly Hills: Sage Publications.

Lee, R. B.
  1979 *The !Kung San: Men, Women, and Work in a Foraging Society*. Cambridge: Cambridge University Press.
  1986 Reflections on Primitive Communism. Paper presented at the International Conference on Hunting and Gathering Societies, London, England.

Lee, R. B., and I. DeVore
  1968 *Man the Hunter*. Chicago: Aldine.

Leiderman, P. H., and G. F. Leiderman
  1977 Economic Change and Infant Care in an East African Agricultural Community. In *Culture and Infancy: Variations in the Human Experience*, ed. P. H. Leiderman et al. New York: Academic Press.

LeVine, R. A.
  1977 Child Rearing as Cultural Adaptation. In *Culture and Infancy: Variations in the Human Experience*, ed. P. H. Leiderman et al. New York: Academic Press.
  1989 Human Parental Care: Universal Goals, Cultural Strategies, Individual Behavior. In *Parental Behavior in Diverse Societies*, ed. R. A. LeVine, P. M. Miller and M. M. West. San Francisco, Calif.: Jossey-Bass.

Lewin, R.
  1986 Damage to Tropical Forests or Why Were There So Many Kinds of Animals? *Science* 473:149–50.

Lovejoy, C. O.
  1981 The Origin of Man. *Science* 211:341–50.

Low, B. S.
  1978 Environment Uncertainty and the Parental Strategies of Marsupials and Placentals. *American Naturalist* 112:197–213.

Mackey, W. C.
  1985 *Fathering Behaviors: The Dynamics of the Man-Child Bond*. New York: Plenum.

Malinowski, B.
1929   *The Sexual Life of Savages in Northwestern Melanesia.* London: George Routledge.

McCreedy, M.
1990   The Arms of the Dibouka. Paper presented at the International Conference on Hunting and Gathering Societies, Fairbanks, Alaska.

Mead, M.
1935   *Sex and Temperment.* New York: Morrow.

Melancon, T. F.
1981   Marriage and Reproduction Among the Yanomamo Indians of Venezuela. Ph.D. diss. Pennsylvania State University, University Park.

Moise, R.
1987   Good Blood: Hunting Ritual of the Biaka Pygmies. Paper presented at the American Anthropological Association Meetings, Chicago, Illinois.

Mortimer, J. T., and J. London
1984   The Varying Linkages of Work and Family. In *Work and Family: Changing Roles of Men and Women,* ed. Patricia Voydanoff. Palo Alto, Calif.: Mayfield.

Mukhopadhyay, C. C.
1983   Beyond Babies and Brawn: Rethinking the Sexual Division of Labor in the Family. Unpublished ms.

Mukhopadhyay, C. C., and P. J. Higgins
1988   Anthropological Studies of Women's Status Revisited: 1977–1987. *Annual Reviews in Anthropology* 17:461–95.

Munroe, R. H., and R. L. Munroe
1971   Household Density and Infant Care in an East African Society. *Journal of Social Psychology* 83:3–13.

1989   Father's Role in Four Societies. Paper presented at the American Anthropological Association Meetings, Washington, D.C.

Murdock, G. P.
1949   *Social Structure.* New York.

Murdock, G. P., and C. Provost
1973   Factors in the Division of Labor by Sex: A Cross-Cultural Analysis. *Ethnology* 12:203–25.

Neuwelt-Truntzer, S.
   1981   Ecological Influences on the Physical, Behavioral and Cognitive
           Development of Pygmy Children. Ph.D. diss., University of
           Chicago.

Ortner, S. B.
   1974   Is Female to Male as Nature is to Culture? In *Woman, Culture
           and Society*, ed. M. Z. Rosaldo and L. Lamphere. Stanford,
           Calif.: Stanford University Press.

Parke, R. D., and S. O'Leary
   1976   Family Interaction in the Newborn Period: Some Findings,
           Some Observations and Some Unsolved Issues. In *The Develop-
           ing Individual in a Changing World*, ed. K. Riegan and J.
           Meacham. The Hague: Moulton.

Parke, R. D., and D. B. Sawin
   1980   The Family in Early Infancy: Social Interactional and Attitudinal
           Analyses. In *The Father-Infant Relationship*, ed. F. A. Peder-
           sen. New York: Praeger.

Parke, R. D., K. Grossmann and B. R. Tinsley
   1981   Father-Mother-Infant Interaction in the Newborn Period: A Ger-
           man-American Comparison. In *Culture and Early Interactions*,
           ed. Tiffany M. Field, Anita M. Sostek, Peter Vietze, and P.
           Herbert Leiderman. Hillsdale, N.J.: Erlbaum.

Parsons, T., and R. F. Bales
   1955   *Family, Socialization and Interaction Process*. Glencoe, Ill.:
           Free Press.

Peacock, N. R.
   1985   Time Allocation, Work and Fertility Among Efe Pygmy Women
           of Northeast Zaire. Ph.D. diss., Harvard University.

Pedersen, F. A., B. J. Anderson, and R. L. Cain
   1980   Parent-Infant and Husband-Wife Interactions Observed at Age
           Five Months. In *The Father-Infant Relationship*, ed. F. A. Ped-
           ersen. New York: Praeger.

Pennetti, V., L. Sgaramella-Zonta, and P. Astolfi
   1986   General Health of the African Pygmies of the Central African
           Republic. In *African Pygmies*, ed. L. L. Cavalli-Sforza. New
           York: Academic Press.

Pennington, R., and H. Harpending
1988 Fitness and Fertility among Kalahari !Kung. *American Journal of Physical Anthropology* 77:303–20.

Phillipson, D. W.
1980 L'Expansion Bantoue en Afrique Orientale et Meridionale: Les Temoignages de l'Archeologie et de la Linguistique. In *L'Expansion Bantoue*, Vol. 2, ed. L. Bouquiaux. Paris: Selaf.

Radcliffe-Brown, A. R.
1924 The Mother's Brother in South Africa. *South African Journal of Science* 21:542–55.

Radin, N.
1981 The Role of the Father in Cognitive, Academic and Intellectual Development. In *The Role of the Father in Child Development*. 2d. ed. Ed. Michael E. Lamb. New York: John Wiley and Sons.

Rasa, O. A. E.
1986 Parental Care in Carnivores. In *Parental Behaviour*, ed. W. Sluckin and M. Herbert. New York: Basil Blackwell.

Richards, P. R.
1973 The Tropical Rainforest. *Scientific American* 229(6): 58–67.

Rosaldo, M. Z.
1974 Woman, Culture and Society: A Theoretical Overview. In *Woman, Culture and Society*, ed. M. Z. Rosaldo and L. Lamphere. Stanford, Calif.: Stanford University Press.

Rosaldo, M. Z., and L. Lamphere, eds.
1974 *Woman, Culture and Society*. Stanford, Calif.: Stanford University Press.

Schebesta, P.
1933 *Among Congo Pygmies*. London: Hutchison and Co.

Schneider, D. M.
1961 The Distinctive Features of Matrilineal Descent Groups. In *Matrilineal Kinship*, ed. David M. Schneider and Kathleen Gough. Berkeley: University of California Press.

Sears, R. R.
1970 Relation of Early Socialization Experiences to Self-Concepts and Gender Role in Middle Childhood. *Child Development* 41:267–89.

References Cited

Siegman, A. W.
1966 Father-Absence During Childhood and Antisocial Behavior. *Journal of Abnormal Psychology* 71:71–74.

Smuts, B. B.
1985 *Sex and Friendship in Baboons*. Hawthorne, N.Y.: Aldine.

Stanley, H. M.
1891 *In Darkest Africa*. 2 vols. New York: Scribners.

Stephens, W. N.
1963 *The Family in Cross-Cultural Perspective*. New York: Holt, Rinehart and Winston.

Strassmann, B. I.
1981 Sexual Selection, Paternal Care, and Concealed Ovulation in Humans. *Ethology and Sociobiology* 2:31–40.

Super, C. M., and S. Harkness
1982 The Development of Affect in Infancy and Early Childhood. In *Cultural Perspectives on Child Development*, ed. D. A. Wanger and H. W. Stevenson. San Francisco, Calif.: Freeman.

Symons, D.
1978 *Play and Aggression: A Study of Rhesus Monkeys*. New York: Columbia University Press.

Taub, D. M.
1985 *Primate Paternalism*. New York: Van Nostrand Reinhold.

Trevathan, W. R.
1987 *Human Birth: An Evolutionary Perspective*. Hawthorne, N.Y.: Aldine.

Trivers, R.
1972 Parental Investment and Sexual Selection. In *Sexual Selection and the Descent of Man*, ed. B. Campbell. Chicago: Aldine.

Turnbull, C. M.
1961 *The Forest People*. New York: Simon and Schuster.
1965a The Mbuti Pygmies: An Ethnographic Survey. *Anthropological Papers of the American Museum of Natural History* 50(3):141–282.
1965b *Wayward Servants: The Two Worlds of the African Pygmies*. Garden City, N.Y.: Natural History Press.
1978 The Politics of Non-Aggression. In *Learning Non-Aggression*, ed. Ashley Montague. New York: Oxford University Press.

1981   Mbuti Womanhood. In *Woman the Gatherer,* ed. Frances Dahlberg. New Haven, Conn.: Yale University Press.

1983   *The Mbuti Pygmies: Change and Adaptation.* New York: Holt, Rinehart and Winston.

Tyson, E.

1894   *A Philological Essay Concerning the Pygmies of the Ancients.* London: David Nutt.

van de Koppel, J. M. H.

1983   *A Developmental Study of the Biaka Pygmies and the Bangandu.* Lisse: Swets and Seitlinger.

van Noten, F.

1982   *The Archaeology of Central Africa.* Austria: Akademische Druck - u. Verlagsanstalt Graz.

Walker, P., and B. S. Hewlett

1989   Artificial Tooth Modification among Central African Pygmies and Bantu. Paper presented at the American Association of Physical Anthropologists Meetings, San Diego, California.

1990   Dental Health and Social Organization Among African Pygmies and Bantu. *American Anthropologist* 92(2):383–98.

Weisner, T. S., and R. Gallimore

1977   My Brother's Keeper: Child and Sibling Caretaking. *Current Anthropology* 18(2):169–90.

Weiss, K.

1973   Demographic Models for Anthropology. Memoirs of the Society for American Archaelogy, No. 27, *American Antiquity* 38(2).

West, M. M., and M. J. Konner

1976   The Role of Father in Anthropological Perspective. In *The Role of the Father in Child Development.* 2nd ed. Ed. Michael E. Lamb. New York: John Wiley and Sons.

Whiting, B. B.

1965   Sex Identity Conflict and Physical Violence: A Comparative Study. *American Anthropologist* 67:123–40.

Whiting, B. B. and J. W. M. Whiting

1975   *Children of Six Cultures.* Cambridge, Mass.: Harvard University Press.

Wilson, E. O.

1975   *Sociobiology: The New Synthesis.* Cambridge, Mass.: Harvard University Press.

Wilson, M., and M. Daly
  1985 Competitiveness, Risk Taking, and Violence: The Young Male Syndrome. *Ethology and Sociobiology* 6:59–73.
Winn, S., G. A. Morelli, and E. Z. Tronick
  1990 The Infant in the Group: A look at Efe Caretaking Practices. *The Cultural Context of Infancy*, ed. J. K. Nugent, B. M. Lester, and T. B. Brazelton. New Jersey: Ablex.
Witkin, H. A., and J. Berry
  1975 Psychological Differentiation in Cross-Cultural Perspective. *Journal of Cross-Cultural Psychology* 6:4–87.
Woodburn, J.
  1968 Introduction to Hadza Ecology. In *Man the Hunter*, ed. R. B. Lee and I. DeVore. Chicago: Aldine.
Yogman, M. W.
  1982 Observations on the Father-Infant Relationship. In *Theory and Research in Behavioral Pediatrics*, ed. B. M. Fitzgerald and M. W. Yogman. New York: Plenum.
Zelditch, M.
  1955 Role Differentialtion in the Nuclear Family. In *Family, Socialization and Interaction Process*, ed. T. Parsons and R. Bales. Glencoe, Ill.: Free Press.

Index

JUNIATA COLLEGE

2820 9100 032 245 6

WITHDRAWN FROM
JUNIATA COLLEGE LIBRARY